KU-418-032

FISH AND FISHERMEN

FISH AND FISHERMEN

Text by Stanislav Lusk
Photographs by Jiří Vostradovský

SUNBURST BOOKS

520671

MORAY DISTRICT COUNCIL

DEPARTMENT OF

LEISURE AND LIBRARIES

79912

English language edition first published 1995
by Sunburst Books, Deacon House, 65 Old Church Street, London SW3 5BS

© Aventinum, Prague 1990
First published by Artia, Prague 1986

Text by Stanislav Lusk
Photographs by Jiří Vostradovský
Translated by Elizabeth Kindlová
Line drawings by Věra Hlavová
Graphic design by Miloš Lang

All rights reserved. No part of this publication may be reproduced, stored in a retrieval system or transmitted, in any form or by any means, electronic, mechanical, photocopying, recording or otherwise, without the prior permission of the copyright holder.

ISBN 1 85778 097 3
Printed in Slovakia by Polygraf
3/20/02/51-01

CONTENTS

WATER AND FISH

Man's interest in fish is as old as mankind itself. Fishing is as much a practical pursuit as pleasurable; for some it is a passion and a pastime, for others a craft or a source of food. However, all fishermen are united by their love of water and their close relationship with it and its aquatic inhabitants. His interest in fish has drawn man to the aquatic world, awakened his curiosity and driven him to explore the underwater population. Fishing holds many surprises in the form of defeats and victories. For the angler it is not important how many fish he catches. A true angler can experience greater joy in catching one fish under certain circumstances than catching ten carp. A true angler should also be interested in the world hidden beneath the water surface and everything which affects the existence and life of fish.

Life on our planet first appeared many millions of years ago in water. Although many forms of life gradually moved into dry land, others remained faithful to the cradle of life – water. Fish represent the largest group of vertebrates whose permanent home is water. Over the course of about 400 million years of evolution these cold-blooded creatures have been able to adapt perfectly, in many different forms, to survive in the water environment. Fish are encountered in almost all water courses – salt, brackish and fresh – in stagnant and flowing waters, in sea and ocean depths and also in high mountain torrents as well as inland lakes and rivers.

The Water Environment

Man has been interested in fish since ancient times, and, over many hundreds of years, has gradually increased his knowledge about fish, their life, breeding and fishing. It was also necessary for man to learn about their environment, because fish rely on water to survive throughout their life. The type of water environment, the quality of the water and its physical and chemical properties are all factors which determine the existence of the many diverse species of fish. Unlike mammals, fish do not possess an effective internal thermoregulative system, so their body temperature is determined by the surrounding water temperature – they are known as poikilothermal creatures. The water temperature plays a decisive role in fish life – it controls the intensity of their metabolism and conditions their bio-

logical activities (e.g. spawning, feeding, migration). Different species of fish have different water temperature requirements which means that we can divide them into two basic groups. Cold-water fish (e.g. Trout, Rainbow Trout, Charr, Grayling, Brook Trout, Huchen, Houting, Miller's Thumb, etc.) survive best at a water temperature of 8–15°C. The second group consists of warm-water (thermophilic) fish (e.g. Carp, European Catfish, Grass Carp, Pike, etc.) which do best at water temperatures of 20–28°C. However, some fish do not have any specific water temperature requirements, which means that they are able to live in any type of waters. These are fish such as the Roach, Burbot, Chub, Pike-perch, Perch and Common Gudgeon.

Water is most dense at a temperature of 4°C, so even if the surface is frozen, the water at the bottom is higher than 0°C which enables fish to survive in the winter. The temperature is generally the same

An Alpine river, with pure water flowing through a mountain valley, conceals a rich population of Trout and Grayling beneath the water surface.

The water surface of a man-made reservoir provides an ideal environment for a number of fish species and a new fishing ground for anglers.

throughout flowing water, due to the turbulence of the current. In still waters, particularly in deeper reservoirs, temperature stratification occurs. In winter the water is warmest at the bottom, in spring the water mixes and in summer it is then warmest at the surface and coldest at the bottom of the reservoir or lake. In autumn the water layers remix and the water temperature is stratified again to its winter state. A knowledge of the dynamics of water temperature masses enables anglers to increase their chances of success, because fish will remain in those layers where the temperature is best for them.

The intensity of the current is also very important to the life of the fish. We can divide water courses into two basic groups – flowing waters (brooks, streams, rivers) and still waters (lakes, pools, reservoirs, fishponds, etc.). The speed of the current in flowing waters is determined primarily by the height of the incline of the riverbed, as

9

The clear pure water of a mountain stream trickles peacefully between the smooth stones and boulders, and it is difficult to believe that, with the coming of spring, it will change into a fast and savage torrent.

◄
Just the time spent at the waterside provides anglers with some wonderful moments regardless of whether or not they catch anything.

well as by its width and by the depth of the water course. Water currents are strongest in rapids which then pass into stretches with a constant current and calm pools. During the course of long-term evolution the different species of fish have adapted to variations in current intensity in such a way that we can recognize the typical inhabitants of flowing and still waters. The body structure, in particular, of the typical current-loving species has adapted to life in fast-flowing water – these are fish of the Trout, Grayling and Barbel species. But there are also other fish to be found in flowing water which do not like currents. These are species living downstream in the so-called 'Bream' zone. Apart from temperatures and currents, fish life is also affected by other physical water properties, mainly density and viscosity as well as the water's permeability to sun-rays and light.

The most important chemical property of water is its content of dissolved oxygen. Oxygen is indispensable in that it enables fish and other aquatic organisms to breathe, and it also promotes the decay of organic matter, forming a significant link in the food cycle in water. While the oxygen content in the air is more or less constant, its content changes in water and is dependent on the temperature – e.g. at 5°C water at 100% saturation contains 12.9 mg oxygen per litre, at 25°C it is only 8.6 mg oxygen per litre. The most important sources of oxygen in water are green algae and plants which produce it by photosynthesis. Oxygen also enters the water by diffusion from the air (by waves, ripples, etc.). The immediate oxygen content dissolved in water is actually the result of two processes – on the one hand, there is the direct oxygen supply into the water and on the other, the oxygen consumption. All water creatures consume oxygen in water,

11

whether invertebrates – zooplankton, water insect larvae, beetles, molluscs, etc. – or vertebrates, of which the most prominent are fish. Requirements with regard to the oxygen content in water vary according to the species of fish. Highly demanding species of fish such as the Trout, Grayling and Miller's Thumb require at least 5-6 mg of oxygen per litre, those with an average requirement, e.g. the Carp, Common Bream and Roach, can withstand the 1.2-3 mg limit, and undemanding species such as the Crucian Carp, Goldfish, Tench and Weatherfish can survive even if the oxygen content falls to 0.5-1 mg per litre. The oxygen requirements of fish also depend on the water temperature which affects the metabolism of fish organisms. At higher temperatures fish require and consume more oxygen in the water. In winter when the metabolism level is at its lowest in fish organisms most species survive with less oxygen in the water.

Oxygen in water is also consumed in the biochemical decay of or-

The wide riverbed, dammed by a weir, creates specific conditions; above the weir the calm water which rages and gushes when overflowing, reverts to a flowing river current below the weir.

Fish can even be found living here in these park lakes.

ganic matter. It is this process which, nowadays, as most of our rivers are polluted by much organic waste, frequently causes the fatal asphyxiation of fish. The decaying process of organic matter drains all the soluble oxygen resources in water. Water pollution by organic matter is one of the most serious problems currently restricting fish life in open waters.

A silhouette of the Pike *(Esox lucius)* beneath the water surface gives an idea of the power and predatory instincts concealed in its body.

The reaction of water - acid or alkaline - is another significant chemical factor. This reaction is indicated by the pH value which represents the concentration of hydrogen ions. Most fish have no difficulty living in water with a pH ranging between 6.0-8.5. Higher or lower pH values can have a damaging effect on fish sometimes even causing them to die. At present, particularly due to the fallout of gaseous emissions in rainfall (i.e. acid rain) in a number of regions in Europe (Scandinavia, Denmark, former Czechoslovakia), open waters are becoming acidified - water courses and lakes where the pH falls as low as 3.0-5.0 in value. As a result most species of fish have become extinct in such waters. Only the Brook Trout *(Salvelinus fontinalis)*, which can withstand relatively acid waters, is left as the sole inhabitant of waters with a low pH value.

Of the other chemical substances which may be found in water, the most significant as far as fish life is concerned are hydrogen sulphide and ammonia. Hydrogen sulphide occurs with the decay of proteinaceous substances due to the lack of oxygen and is toxic for fish. Ammonia, which is normally found in NH_4 form, does not harm fish, but if it occurs in water in NH_3 form, even a low concentration (1-2 mg per litre) kills fish.

A very significant role in the water environment is played by certain elements which are classed as nutrients - primarily nitrogen and phosphorus. These substances directly or indirectly affect the water environment including the plant and animal organisms living there. Human activity has been the main cause of the complex process known as eutrophication but a significant role is also played by nu-

The sun, green algae and plants produce an abundance of oxygen which may create a foam in which each tiny bubble is formed from life-giving oxygen.

The coming spring has not only awakened the river branch, from which the blanket of ice has disappeared, but also the surrounding plant world.

trients. Eutrophication is the term for a whole series of changes occurring in the water environment which diminish the quality of the water. The eutrophication process in fresh waters has already become a major problem, threatening the water quality in most water systems.

In the past the properties and character of the water environment were the result of the action of natural factors. Nowadays the properties and character of water are determined mainly by human activity, which is, unfortunately, usually damaging to the environment. In many cases the quality of the water has become so poor that fish life cannot be supported.

The Adaptation of Fish to the Water Environment

Fish are perfectly adapted to life in the water environment both in the structure of their bodies and in their biological functions. Their adaptation has become synonymous with a certain level of perfec-

The head of the male Trout *(Salmo trutta)* with its hooked lower jaw distinguishes it from the female.

tion, as indicated by the comparison – 'like a fish in water' – when expressing perfection, harmony with the environment, utilization of resources, etc.

The shape of a fish reveals much about its way of life. Fish living in flowing waters have a fusiform body (e.g. salmonids – *Salmonidae*), whereas fish in calm waters have a flat-sided, high body (e.g. the

This view of the head of the Barbel shows a mouth with massive fleshy lips which are capable of over-turning stones when searching for food. There is a pair of groping barbels on the top and bottom lips of the mouth.

16

It is clear when looking at the open jaws of the Pike *(Esox lucius)* that it is a predator, capable of swallowing prey hardly any smaller than itself.

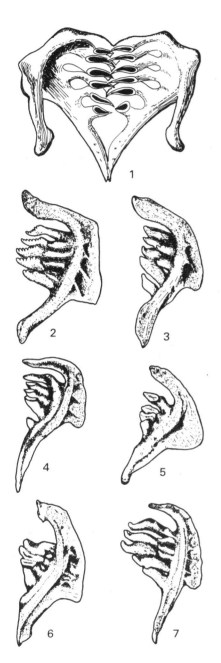

In cyprinid fish *(Cyprinidae)* the fifth pair of branchial arches are transformed into so-called pharyngeal bones or teeth. The shape and arrangement of these teeth is characteristic of each individual species. 1 - a set of pharyngeal teeth of the Nase *(Chondrostoma nasus)*, 2 - the pharyngeal teeth of the Rudd *(Scardinius erythrophthalmus)*, 3 - the Silver Bream *(Blicca bjoerkna)*, 4 - the Common Bream *(Abramis brama)*, 5 - the Tench *(Tinca tinca)*, 6 - the Crucian Carp *(Carassius carassius)*, 7 - the Orfe *(Leuciscus idus)*.

Roach and Common Bream). Fish dwelling on the river bed (benthonic) have a flat belly and a wide body (the Miller's Thumb, Barbel). Predators (the Pike, Pike-perch) have arrow or wedge-shaped heads. Other species of fish living in hiding places on the river bed have a serpentine body (the European Eel, Weatherfish, Stone Loach).

Likewise the shape of the head and position of the mouth (terminal, superior or dorsal, inferior or ventral) in different species of fish corresponds to their way of life and methods of gathering food. Fish collecting food from the bed (e.g. the Carp, Barbel, Bream) have ventral mouths. Predators have terminal mouths which open up broadly with toothed jaws. In cyprinid fishes *(Cyprinidae)* the teeth are located on the 5th branchial arch – the so-called gullet teeth used to crush the incoming food. Some fish have barbels around the mouth (e.g. the Barbel, Carp, European Catfish etc.) serving as an organ for taste and touch. The Catfish moves its long barbels to lure other inquisitive fish and then seizes them as its prey. The dorsal mouth is found in fish that collect food from the water course or surface.

The gills are important organs which act as lungs in fish thereby ensuring the appropriate exchange of gases. The gills are located in the gill cavity of the head and covered with flat bones – gill covers *(opercula)*. The red coloured gills are placed on the outer side of the first four branchial arches. The gill tissue is interwoven with a thick net of fine capillary vessels and carbon dioxide, ammonia and any other metabolism waste from the blood flow through these vessels and are released into the water. Oxygen from the water penetrates the fine epithelium of gill leaflets where it is dissolved. The gills have to be rinsed with water constantly in order to ensure their proper function.

The water is sucked through the mouth and mouth cavity with the movement of the gill covers which work like a pump and then the water is released through the gill gaps. In some species other organs and tissue such as the skin, intestine and swim-bladder are also important for breathing as they complement the function of the gills.

Fish have fins in place of limbs to stabilize them and propel them through the water. There are two pairs of fins – pectoral and ventral fins. Fish also have three odd, unpaired fins – the caudal, dorsal and anal fins. The caudal fin in some fish is shaped like an oar (e.g. the Catfish, Burbot), but in most fish it looks like a fork. The caudal fin together with the back part of the body is the main source of movement of the fish in water. In some fish (e.g. the Perches – *Percidae* family) the dorsal fin is divided into two parts. The anal fin acts like the keel of a ship, maintaining the vertical position of the fish in water. The shape of the fin, its position and the number of rays in the fins is significant for distinguishing individual species of fish.

The skin covering the fish's body consists of an outer protective cover, which can also fulfil another function (exchange of gases, sense perception). Fish skin is smooth and bald with an abundance of leathery mucous glands. These are pigment cells in the skin which create the colouring of fishes. The colouring within one species depends on the specific fish, on the surroundings, the sex, season of the year, age and condition. The basic colours of fish are black, yellow or red and further colours result from a combination of these basic colours.

It is very unusual to encounter such a variation on the normal colouring, such as in the case of this albino European Catfish *(Silurus glanis)*. ▶

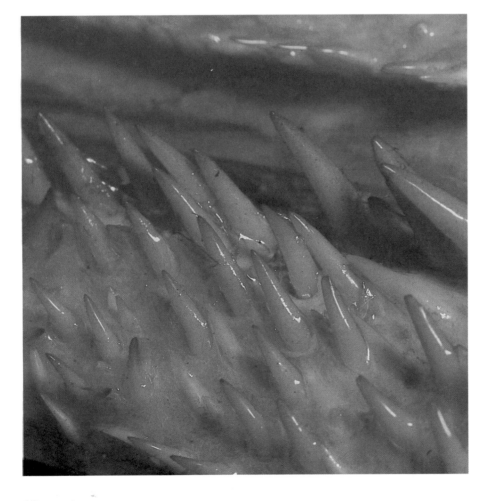

The dangerous teeth of the Pike.

The silvery lustre of fish, particularly on the belly sections, is caused by guanidine crystals found in the pigment cells which break up or reflect light rays.

The skin of most fish contains characteristic horn formations – scales – which increase the protective function of the skin. Only some species of European ichthyofauna have no scales – e.g. the European Catfish, Miller's Thumb, Stone Loach, Weatherfish, etc. Scales are arranged on the fish's body in such a way as not to restrict its movement. The scales increase with the growth of the fish and their structure is typical of that particular species.

Scales are a sort of personal identity card of each fish recording the most important moments and events in a fish's life. If scales can be 'read' much can be learnt of the life of a caught fish. Above all, scales can determine which species the fish belongs to, how old it is or when it was born. We can learn under what conditions a fish has lived during the past year, when it had enough food and when it did not, when it matured and when it spawned. The scales can also indicate how it grew over the years, what length it grew to and what weight it reached. Hence the reading of fish scales can provide us with a great deal of knowledge about the fish's life.

The fish's actual body consists of a supporting skeleton and body musculature. The skeleton primarily consists of a skull and backbone, then the skeleton of individual fins, gills and so-called little muscle bones. The muscles are used for the movement of the entire fish in the water as well as for the movement of the individual organs and body parts (mouth, fins, gill-covers, etc.). The fish musculature is of special importance to people as a form of food. Fish meat is very healthy and, from the point of view of healthy nutrition, consumption of it is far too low.

The coordination and motor function of a fish's organism and its perception of the surrounding world, impulses and reactions are fulfilled by the nervous system and glands with internal secretion. The nervous system consists of both the brain and spinal cord which drive the motor functions, as well as an autonomous section which deals with the receipt of impulses, the execution of functions, enervation of the individual parts of the body, etc. The internal secretion glands produce hormones which operate and influence the development of the fish organism. So, for example, the thyroid gland produces the hormone influencing the development of fish

The Carp *(Cyprinus carpio)*, the bald (scale-less) carp form. The scales are distributed irregularly over the body, most of which is scaleless.

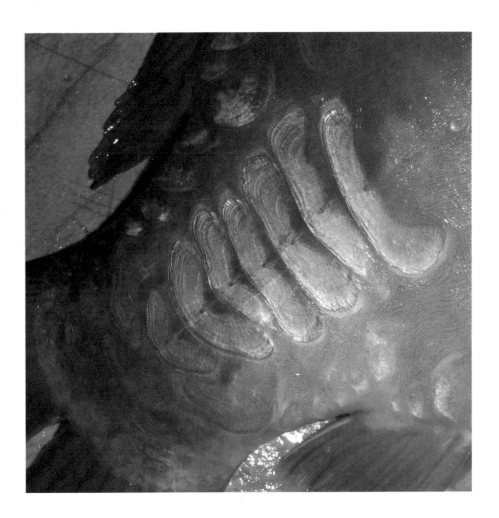

◄
Scales cover the fish's body in the same way that tiles cover a roof, providing it with firm and flexible protection.

in the first period of their life. The pancreas produces the hormone which influences the consumption of oxygen in the body. The thymus affects the growth of the fish and its functions throughout its entire life. Growth in fish, unlike that of higher vertebrates, is not limited. In fishing practice, hormones of the hypophysis – the pituitary gland – can be used in artificial fish spawning.

The sense organs and their sensors provide fish with a sense of direction in water and enable them to react to external occurrences. Fish are basically myopic creatures and can barely see beyond a distance of 5–10 metres. However, they have a broad field of vision. The eye of a fish appears to be numb, because it does not have a lid and the fish moves it as little as possible. Most fish have relatively big eyes; only those species which are active at night or live in shelters during the day (the European Eel, Burbot, European Catfish) have small eyes. The sense of sight is complemented by other senses. The taste buds, which pick up substances dissolved in water, are found in the pair of nostrils situated on a fish's head. They are also found in the mouth cavity, on the barbels, around the mouth and on the body surface. The fish's strong sense of taste can be confirmed by the experience of fishermen who commonly use soluble substances as bait.

The centre of sound perception and the centre of balance is situated in the membraneous labyrinth found in the skull. Sounds are perceived as shocks or water oscillation. Some fish also emit sounds themselves - for example, the Rainbow Trout, the Weatherfish or Spined Loach. The swim-bladder in fish is mainly used

as a hydrostatic organ. It is found in the body cavity under the spine and is shaped like a single or double-chamber pouch. The swim-chamber enables fish to 'rise' in a water course and to stay at a certain depth by providing the counter-pressure to the pressure of the water course, thereby preventing the deformation of the fish's body. The content of the swim-bladder is mainly made up of hydrogen, then, to a lesser extent, oxygen and carbon dioxide and, in rare cases, other gases as well. The pressure in the swim-bladder changes slowly and gradually. If a fish is caught at a great depth and quickly pulled out, e.g. from 20–25 m to the surface, its swim-bladder expands and often bursts, and a flat Bream, for instance, suddenly inflates like a ball. The Miller's Thumb *(Cottus gobio)* does not have a swim-bladder and, therefore, it does not swim in water but moves about in leaps and bounds from shelter to shelter on the river bed.

An important sense organ in fish is the system of lateral lines which function in fish like radar and provide fish with a sense of direction

The eye of the Rainbow Trout – a detail shot shows the magnificent range of colours and refutes the somewhat derogatory term of 'fish eye'.　▶

The unusual colouring of the Brook Trout *(Salvelinus fontinalis)* makes it one of the most beautiful fish in our waters.
◄

even if they cannot see – e.g. in the dark or in cloudy water. It registers the movement of other objects or creatures in the water surrounding the fish and records water oscillation. Even blind fish are able to survive if their system of lateral lines is in good working order. Cases are known of blind pike which even attack artificial angling baits.

The blood system ensures the transportation of substances and products required for the metabolism or of the resulting substances. It is made up of a system of blood vessels, the heart, which functions like a single-chamber pump, and blood. Blood only makes up about a fiftieth of a fish's body weight which is a relatively small amount. The blood of certain species of fish (e.g. the European Eel) contains protein elements which are toxic to human tissue and can cause inflammation in sensitive people. The toxic effect of the blood can be eliminated at a temperature of more than 70°C. The lymph fluid which flows in the lymphatic vessels fulfils an intermediary function between the blood and body tissues.

The digestive system of fish is relatively simple. It begins at the mouth cavity and passes into a short gullet. In predators (the Pike, Pike-perch, European Catfish) the mouth cavity is usually toothed. Fish that feed on plankton are equipped with gills surrounding the gullet cavity which form a sort of filtration system – a sieve which strains and captures plankton organisms in fish (cyprinid – *Cyprinidae*) which have gullet teeth on the 5th branchial arch that

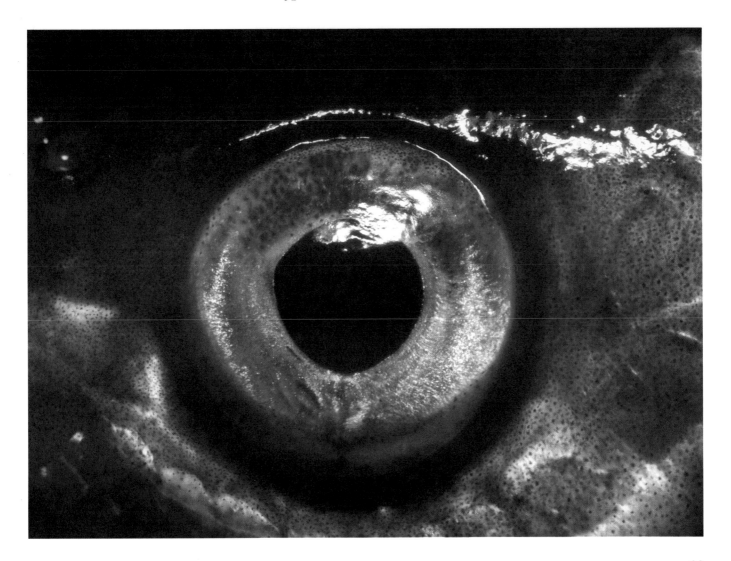

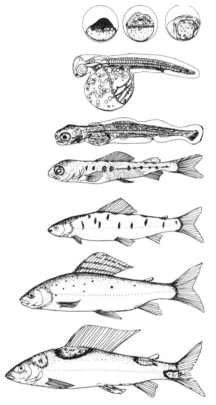

The gills of the Pike *(Esox lucius)*, the organ in a fish which ensures a substantial part of the exchange of gases (oxygen, carbon dioxide, ammonia) between the fish's body and the surrounding water.

crush food. The gullet is very short and passes into the stomach which is very elastic in predatory fish. Other species (e.g. the Carp, Common Bream, etc.) do not possess this part of the digestive tract. Wormy so-called pyloric protuberances, which increase the intestinal area, are found between the stomach and intestine in salmonids or gadoid fishes. The actual intestine is a relatively simple tube which varies in length.

Predator fish have a shorter intestine than omnivorous or herbivorous fish. The intestine passes out of an opening from the stomach cavity in front of the anal fin. In fish the function of two large glands – the pancreas and liver – is connected with the digestive tract. The products of the pancreas and liver contribute to the digestion of food in the intestine.

Dark red kidneys are situated in the stomach cavity under the spine from where urine passes through the ureter and out of the anal orifice. The stomach cavity in fish also contains the sex glands; in males these are the testicles producing the sperm cells, in females the ovaries where the eggs form, which, in fish, are called spawn. During the reproduction process called spawning, the mature sex cells are discharged by the male and female. Fertilization occurs in the water once the spawn joins with the sperm.

Fish are among those creatures which do not take care of their offspring after the fertilization of the eggs - or spawn. The amount of spawn released by the female fish is huge; in the Carp it is hundreds to a million eggs, in the Burbot it is also hundreds of thousands, and in most cyprinid fish the number of eggs spawned by one female

The life of the fish can be divided into five periods. The embryonal and larval period is dominated by the processes and changes in the qualitative character forming the individual organs and systems. During the juvenile period the body becomes covered in scales and this period ends with the fish reaching adulthood. The period of adulthood is characterized by the active part taken in the reproduction process. The intensity of growth gradually decreases and the increase in weight starts to prevail over the growth in length. The period of old age is characterized by the gradual reduction in the ability to reproduce, right up to its complete loss and the weakening of the organism which eventually causes death.

24

The artificial spawning of fish. The fertilization of Brook Trout eggs with the milt of the male fish.

amounts to at least hundreds of thousands. Hence even if there are enormous losses during the course of the development of spawn and hatched fish, the reproduction of the species is still secured. Fishes with lower fertility (e.g. salmonids) lay their spawn into some sort of hollow (redd) at the bottom of rivers and cover it with a layer of sand and gravel. Although fish do not possess the parental instinct, they do at least try to choose the most suitable conditions for the development of the fertilized spawn. Therefore most species of fish embark on a journey before they find the most suitable place – the spawning ground. For example, the Nase seek out thresholds of rapids with the suitable quality of water and sometimes they travel several kilometres to reach such places. The European ichthyofauna includes species such as the Salmon, Sea Trout and the Common Sturgeon which travel hundreds of kilometres to get to the spawning ground and reproduce their offspring.

Fish reproduction is carried out according to season. The autumn months are the spawning time of cold-water fish, such as the Trout, Brook Trout or Houting. An exception in the fish world is the Burbot which reproduces in winter. The Pike spawns in early spring when there is still drift-ice on riverbanks. It is followed by the Rainbow Trout, the Huchen, Grayling, Perch and Pike-perch; then most of the remaining species of fish, particularly of the Carp *(Cyprinidae)* family and the Roach and Rudd spawn in May and June. Some species spawn in pairs – e.g. the Pike-perch, European Catfish, Grayling or Huchen. Most species like the Pike, Trout, Tench or Barbel spawn in smaller groups consisting of one female and several males. Fishes in Great Britain, prized by many anglers, such as the Rudd, Bleak or Roach, spawn in shoals. Some species are highly conservative about their conditions for reproduction and if they cannot find the suitable site and conditions, they do not spawn (e.g. the Rudd, Chub, Barbel and of course all salmonids). Other species (e.g. the Roach)

Natural spawning of fish is often accompanied by the splashing and spraying of water.

A catch from the river's Bream zone (the Roach, the Perch, the Common Bream and Asp).

The spawn of the Common Bream *(Abramis brama)*, used for creating an artificial spawning ground, decorates the needles of small spruce branches like tiny beads.

adapt their spawning ground requirements and spawn virtually anywhere, particularly on various roots or flooded green trees and shrubs.

The development of a new fish begins with the fertilization of the spawn – i.e. the combination of the egg with the sperm. The development of every fish can be divided into several fundamental periods during which the fish lives its life, gives life to its offspring and waits for its death. More details about the various stages of fish development are provided in the illustration.

The reproduction and development of fish in times when the water environment was virtually undisturbed by man, occurred without any problems. However, human society gradually began to interfere with the environment, so that the living conditions of fish grew worse. The worst effects of man's influence on fish life are occurring in the sphere of reproduction, which means that the continued existence of the highest quality fish is now under threat. Consequently artificial breeding and particularly artificial fish reproduction has become very important in the fishing industry. This is an effective means of compensating for the substantial restriction on natural reproduction in many species of fish. The release of the fry (young fish) acquired from artificial breeding into the original water courses will maintain their fish population at appropriate levels. In a number of areas of the fish industry, artificial reproduction is not only undertaken for the purpose of consumption and production breeding, but it also ensures high fish populations in brooks, rivers, reservoirs and lakes.

The fish habitat at a weir attracts species typical of still water – the Common Pike, the Rudd and Roach – as well as fish of running water – the Chub, etc.　　　▶

A catch of the *Cyprinidae* family from the river's Bream zone.

Sunrise over a lake surface is the symbol of the coming of spring which signals a new lease of life for fish and anglers.

Fish Families

There are many different forms of the water environment, but on the basis of several fundamental properties (e.g. the food chain, temperature, pH, water movement, oxygen content, etc.), these can be divided into certain categories which are characterized by their very similar fish colonies. Species of fish which have similar or compatible demands on the water environment inhabit the same water courses. Certain key characteristics and properties of the water environment play a significant role in determining the species and structure of its fish colony, although, in this respect, the intentional or unintentional influence of man is becoming increasingly important. The influence exerted by the water environment on fish and angling is discussed later in this book.

Every water course is occupied by a particular type of fish colony, which is generally characterized by one basic or extended species, as well as, usually, other secondary species, which are of minor significance from an angling point of view. For example, the Bream family comprises the Carp, Pike, Roach and a whole number of further species as well as the Common Bream. The Brook Trout family, typical of certain lakes in the Alps and northern Europe, is also made up of various species of Whitefishes *(Coregonidae),* in the rivers it is the Trout family and small fishes, mainly the Minnow and Miller's Thumb. The Barbel family, which is found in middle stretches of rivers, is made up of the Chub, Nase, Common Gudgeon and others. The composition of fish families is determined by the effect of the water environment. If we want to interfere with this structure, particularly in open waters, we have to assess the consequences of our intervention. Fish species will survive in a water environment which is suited to their requirements and which provides them with the type of space and food that they need. Although the relationship between water and fish was always an exclusive one in the past, man's influence on natural conditions has meant that the fish too has now become instrumental in modifying the conditions of its water course.

WATER COURSES

A huge network of water courses extends like a cobweb over the earth's surface, modelling, sculpting and refreshing the earth. Water creates valleys through which it flows to its destination – the open sea. Like small capillary vessels, numerous springlets, brooks, streams and rivulets unite to form the river which embraces further tributaries on its route, gaining strength and force until it reaches the estuary, where the opposite riverbank is often out of sight, far across the vast expanse of water. The character and properties of the water course alter significantly during the course of its journey, from the source to the sea, which obviously has an effect on its underwater inhabitants. The speed and force of the water current gradually diminish as the river's downstream gradient decreases. Fast flowing waters and rapids predominate upstream, while in the middle stretch of the river there are calmer stretches with deeper water and downstream there are virtually no rapids. As the speed of the water current diminishes, the rugged appearance of the riverbed also becomes smoother – upstream the river bed consists of stones and gravel, which give way to sandy and loamy sediments further downstream. The clarity and the oxygen levels of the water decrease downstream, while the temperature rises, and the river is generally less clean.

The gradual change in the quality and character of the water, from the source of the river throughout its course, is also reflected in its fish colonies. Some species live upstream, others in the middle stretches or downstream. The number of species populating the river generally increases with the flow. Some types of fish with particular characteristics are so specific to certain stretches of the river that the water course can be divided into so-called fish zones. These fish zones follow one after another, in the direction of the current, in the order: the Trout zone, the Grayling zone, the Barbel zone and the Bream zone. Each zone contains a typical fish colony where species characteristic to that zone as well as other types of fish are found, all of which are best suited to the environment of the zone in question. For example, in the Barbel zone, apart from the representative species, the Barbel *(Barbus barbus)* itself, further typical species also exist – the Chub *(Leuciscus cephalus)*, the Nase *(Chondrostoma nasus)*, the *Alburnoides bipunctatus,* the Dace *(Leuciscus leuciscus)*, the Gudgeon *(Gobio gobio),* and others.

A stream with a waterfall symbolizes trout water courses which are characterized by rapids and clean, cold flowing water – an environment suitable for the Brown Trout *(Salmo trutta m. fario)* and the Brook *(Salvelinus fontinalis)*.

33

Even a brook meandering through meadows can conceal well nourished trout in its waters, because, apart from the normal water food, they also have dry-land food from the surrounding area.

The succession of the individual fish zones may be shifted or, particularly in smaller courses, one zone might be omitted from the succession. Fish zones are often altered as a result of man's interference – e.g. as a result of colder waters released from dams, Trout and Grayling often appear in what were originally Barbel or Bream zones.

A wonderful milt male Trout weighing 3.5 kg with a lower hooked jaw. ▶

The Trout Zone

Water courses inhabited by the Brown Trout *(Salmo trutta fario)* and Grayling *(Thymallus thymallus)* are known as trout waters. These courses can be sub-divided into the Trout zone and Grayling zone. The Grayling zone mainly includes brooks, streams and rivulets, as well as bigger courses. Trout zones contain the cleanest water, therefore the species encountered there are very demanding on water purity but also require sufficient oxygen and do not like water that is too warm (up to 20°C).

The fish colony in trout waters is relatively sparse with regard to the number of species found. The most prolific and the most significant species is the Trout, then to a lesser extent other salmonids such as the Brook Trout *(Salvelinus fontinalis)* and the Rainbow Trout *(Salmo gairdneri)*. The Grayling can also be found in lower stretches of the Trout zone. Other species encountered in trout water include primarily the Miller's Thumb *(Cottus gobio)* and the Alpine Bullhead *(Cottus poecilopus)*, as well as the Minnow *(Phoxinus phoxinus)*. On the continent this zone also contains other types of fish – the Burbot *(Lota lota)* and the Stone Loach *(Noemacheilus barbat-*

ulus). It is often falsely assumed that the Trout zone is only found in the rivers of mountain and hill regions – it also exists in lowland courses. The decisive factor is that the water is clean, flowing, cool and contains sufficient oxygen. Although the Trout is found in the Alps up to heights of about 2,700 m or in the Tatras up to about 1,700 m above sea level, these mountain waters are not an ideal environment for the fish which is indicated by their slow growth. Fishes of the Trout zone find ideal conditions above all in submontane regions or in lowland courses where the growing season is longer, there are more stable current conditions and, most important, an abundance of food.

The nooks and crannies under stones and clusters of aquatic plants (e.g. *Batrachium fluitans, Callitriche palustria, Myriophyllum spicatum,* etc.) provide a home for many zoobenthos – above all the larvae of *Ephemeroptera* (Mayfly), *Plecoptera, Trichoptera, Simuliidae,* as well as the *Astacus fluviatilis* (River Crab) and other water invertebrates which are welcome and nutritious food for fish. There is also plentiful nutrition in trout waters in meadows and fields where, apart from aquatic food, fish also have a rich selection of food sources from dry land.

▶
An artificially formed step in a trout brook forms a suitable environment for bigger fish.

A catch of Trout (*Salmo trutta* - top specimen) and Brook Charr (*Salvelinus fontinalis* - lower specimen).
◄

The typical and most significant species of this zone, the king of brooks and streams on islands and on the European mainland, is the Brown Trout *(Salmo trutta fario)*. The Brown Trout, like the Salmon, originated in the sea but it migrated from the sea to spawn in the uppermost stretches of rivers – the brooks, rivulets and streams. Part of its offspring from the spawned eggs did not return to the sea but remained permanently in its birthplace and created the so-called brook species, like the *Salmo trutta morpha fario,* which is perfectly adapted to life in this water environment. The fusiform, muscular body, ending in a wedge-shaped, blunt head, is well-suited to life in

A Lake Trout *(Salmo trutta m. lacustris)* catch is easier from a motor boat and by means of a dragged trap at great depth.

fast-flowing water and enables the Brown Trout to swim against a current of up to 3 metres per second. The adipose fin, between the dorsal and caudal fin, is a characteristic mark of Brown Trout and salmonids *(Salmonidae)*. The Brown Trout is more varied in shape and colour than other freshwater fish on the European continent. Its back is usually greenish-brown in colour, but can also be yellowish-black, and some fish have a bluish tinge, but there are also further colour nuances. The abdominal part of the body is always lighter, with shades of yellow or off-white. On the back and sides as well as on the dorsal and adipose fin these fish usually have beautiful red spots which, particularly on the sides, are tinged with lighter white or silvery yellow. Some fish may not possess these red marks and merely have dark grey or black spots. Virtually no trout is coloured in exactly the same way as another, as each brook, stream or rivulet contains Brown Trout with their own characteristic colouring.

The Miller's Thumb *(Cottus gobio)* is another typical species of trout brooks and streams; in flowing waters at higher levels it tends to be replaced by its relative, the Alpine Bullhead *(Cottus poecilopus)*.

Because of the great challenge which it poses, fishing in trout brooks is exciting and attractive for every angler.

The Brown Trout leads an individualistic way of life displaying territorial behaviour and defending the domain it has chosen in the water course. The size of this domain is determined by the size of the individual fish as well as the division of the water environment. The borders of the domain are defined by the sight range of the fish. All intruders entering this domain are driven out immediately. For most of the year the Brown Trout remains in its home territory where it has shade and food. The main food of the Brown Trout in a small water course consists of various water insect larvae – *Trichoptera, Ephemeroptera* (Mayfly), *Plecoptera, Odonata* (Dragonfly) as well

39

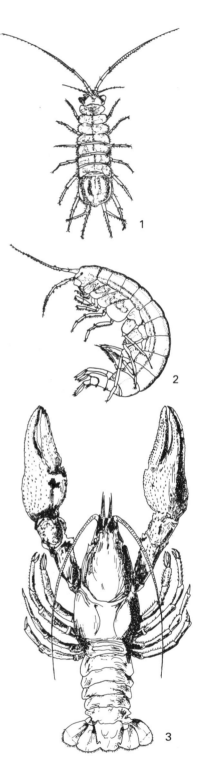

as water molluscs (e.g. Ancylus), various maggots and earthworms and even dry land insects that have fallen into the water. Larger fish will go after small fish for food, and even frogs and mice.

The Brown Trout only lives to a relatively young age (3 – 6 years). Although the growth potential of the Brown Trout is very good, this depends on the size of the water environment it inhabits, the amount of food available and numerous other factors. In brooks and streams it grows to a length of 150 – 250 mm at three years of age. In poor mountain conditions at heights of 1,500 – 1,800 m above sea level it grows very slowly and five year old fish measure a mere 120 – 150 mm. On the contrary, in lowland meadow brooks, where the Brown Trout has sufficient food and water, it reaches a size of 250 – 300 mm at 3 years of age.

The Brown Trout matures at 2 – 4 years of age, males usually a year earlier than females. The Trout reproduces with the onset of cold weather in October to December – sometimes spawning goes on until January. During the spawning season, the Trout leave their home-ground and migrate further upstream and into tributaries. This journey is usually undertaken against the current, and involves overcoming various steps and weirs up to a height of 1.5 m. At the spawning ground the female flaps out a hollow with her fins and body on

Representatives of the larger crustaceans (*Malacostraca*) which are food for fishes: 1 – water ladybird (*Asellus aquaticus*), 2 – sand-hopper (*Gammarus lacustris*), 3 – river crab (*Astacus astacus*).

40

A prison type of trap box for catching female Trout migrating to their spawning grounds in higher stretches of the brook.

The yellow Marigold (*Caltha palustris*) flowers not only announce the advent of spring at a trout brook, but also the beginning of the angling season.

The Brook Trout (*Salvelinus fontinalis*) which was imported into Europe from North America one hundred years ago.

the sandy or gravel bottom of a redd where, with the participation of the male, she spawns mature eggs. There are usually 2,000–3,000 eggs (measuring 5–6 mm) per kg of the female's weight. The development of the fertilized spawn lasts almost all winter and the small Trout fish hatch in 100–200 days.

The Brown Trout is one of the species in which artificial spawning has been carried out for more than 100 years. The fertilized spawn is protected in artificial hatcheries and after it hatches the follicular fry is then reared until the age of 1–2 years when it is returned to open courses. Thanks to artificial breeding, most suitable brooks, rivers and streams are well populated with the Trout and so these waters provide much enjoyment for the angler.

Trout are caught with a landing net when the bait consists of either a spinner or a small dead fish. On larger courses, however, anglers use an artificial fly. Trout fishing methods and any other restrictions, such as the period of protection and the length or size of catch, tend to be regulated by local rules in individual countries. Trout fishing is one of the most appealing forms of angling and trout anglers form a specific category of followers of St. Peter's Guild. Those who have had a taste of the magic of trout fishing, frequently fall under its spell and pursue this pastime for the rest of their life.

Apart from Brown Trout, one also comes across other salmonids in brooks and streams. The most common is probably the Charr *(Salvelinus alpinus)* or the Brook Trout *(Salvelinus fontinalis)* which was imported into Europe 100 years ago from North America. Both species inhabit the running and still waters of northern Europe. The Charr is equal to the Brown Trout in the beauty of its colours. Its back is a mottled olive to bluish-green with lighter sides and an orange to reddish belly. The pectoral, ventral and anal fins are pinkish lined with

Smooth boulders on the bed of a mountain stream show that totally different water often flows this way – wild and fast water which is dangerous to fish and sometimes also to man.

43

The angler often has to wade to the middle of the river in search of fish.

a white and red stripe. Yellow, blue and carmine spots are often also found on the sides and back. It has a relatively big jagged mouth with toothed jaws with a black mouth membrane. The Charr is a really beautiful fish which enhances brooks and the other waters it inhabits.

Its survival requirements and biology are similar to those of the Brown Trout with which it can also reproduce crossbreeds named the 'tiger' fish after its colouring. It possesses a life-saving quality – it can live in waters with relatively low pH values, and so, in many of these waters, which are unfortunately on the increase, it is becoming the sole fish inhabitant.

The Rainbow Trout *(Salmo gairdneri)* is only found on a localized basis in brooks and small rivers. A suitable environment for this species, also from the North American continent, are rivers which have a relatively high water temperature, even in winter, due to the springs rising from the basin. The Rainbow Trout is beautifully coloured, particularly during the reproduction season, and the males boast a stunning rainbow stripe which stretches the length of their sides.

The Grayling *(Thymallus thymallus)* is also found in larger water courses of the Trout zone. Other fish characteristic to trout brooks and streams include the Miller's Thumb *(Cottus gobio)* which in certain regions of Europe replaces the Alpine Bullhead *(Cottus poecilopus)*. The Bullhead has an ugly appearance with its dragon-shaped

A river current flowing over the edge of a weir changing from a calm river into a rush of bubbling and spraying water. ▶

44

head which is virtually flat, large in proportion to the fusiform body. The body is slippery smooth without scales. The Bullhead's body colour is perfectly adapted to its surroundings – the background colour is brown to grey with dark spots – an ideal camouflage. The Bullhead does not have a swim-bladder and moves along the river bed in leaps. It shelters under stones. It lives off tiny larvae of aquatic insects and grows to 150 mm at most but usually to 100 mm. It reproduces in April and May when the female lays her spawn on the stones of the river bed and the male guards the spawn throughout the development period which lasts about 20 days. The harmfulness of the Bullhead is exaggerated by anglers who believe that it eats the trout eggs, but there is no justification for such a view. Bullheads are an important part of fish colonies in brooks and streams because they are sensitive indicators of water purity.

The Brook Trout *(Salvelinus fontinalis)* is capable of living in acidic waters which other fish cannot tolerate.

The Minnow *(Phoxinus phoxinus)* is a small and very beautiful fish and its home are clean brooks with calm waters. It usually grows to 60–80 mm and, in rare cases, to 120 mm. Its colouring is equally as attractive as that of colourful aquarium fish, particularly in the spawning season. Its basic colour is brownish green on the back and the sides are green with a golden lustre, the belly is whitish to pale pinkish in colour. The back and sides have dark spots. During the spawning season (April to July) the mature fish have more distinctive colouring, the males a clear carmine red colour on the front part of the belly, on the edges of the lips, on the base of the paired fins and the anal fin. They have a distinctive spawning rash on their heads. The Minnow lives in shoals and is a fish which merits full protection, especially as it has gradually been disappearing in many countries in central Europe in recent years.

In lowland Trout brooks and rivers, apart from the species already mentioned, one also encounters the Chub *(Leuciscus cephalus)* and sometimes even the Gudgeon *(Gobio gobio)* or other fish that have strayed from the broader stretches of river downstream.

Although Trout courses possess relatively sparse fish life, they are home to the species which are the true jewels of the fish world.

The worst pollution is found in populated areas. ▶

The Grayling Zone

The Trout zone runs into the Grayling zone as the course or river gains in force, begins to meander and, apart from rapids and a few fast-flowing water stretches, forms deeper pools and expanses with slow-flowing water. The calm and rapid waters alternate. The water temperature reaches 20°C in summer and the water becomes slightly more polluted and less nourishing which affects the levels in the food chain. As in the Trout zone, the river banks here lack abundant plant growth, but are rich in diatomaceous fossils and algae (*Batrachium aquatile, Fontinalis antipyretica, Callitriche palustris* and *C. polymorpha,* etc.).

In certain regions of this type of water the Grayling is not found, and these areas are part of the Trout zone. Unlike Trout waters,

Grayling zones are more open and extensive. The Nase *(Chondros-toma nasus)* is frequently the dominant species in Grayling waters in central and eastern Europe (the Carpathians, the Transylvanian Alps). Some anglers refer to this zone as the Nase zone and not the Grayling zone. The fact that the Nase is often spotted in the Grayling zone, particularly during the spawing time, and that the Grayling can be found in the Barbel zone, indicates that these two species have similar environmental requirements. The typical species of this zone is the Grayling *(Thymallus thymallus)*.

The trout type of river where, apart from the Trout and Grayling, one encounters other species from the Barbel zone. The queen of mountain-side rivers – the Huchen *(Hucho hucho)* – also lives there.

◄

In Europe the natural border of the existence of this species is the 45°C of northern latitude. However, the Grayling is found north of this border in most European countries, including Great Britain. As the Grayling inhabits the upper and central parts of water courses with oxygenated water, it is only found in isolated areas in certain regions. Although the Grayling originates in flowing waters, it has adapted to the conditions in certain valley reservoirs where it thrives and often even lives to a greater age than in rivers. The shape of the Grayling's body resembles that of the Whitefish or certain cyprinid fishes, but its more elegant, slim, elongated, torpedo-shaped and more colourful body indicates that it is a pure-bred fish. Its adipose fin signifies that it is related to salmonids. It has a small head with large eyes and a delicate mouth positioned low on the body. The body is covered with relatively large scales. Its back is dark to greyish green or brown and the lighter sides fade into a silvery white belly. At the front of the body, particularly behind the head, the Grayling has relatively large black spots, which are unique to each individual fish. A distinctive mark or, one could say, coat of arms of the Grayling is its dorsal fin, called a banner in male fish. Alternating stripes on the dorsal fin consist of brown, black and brownish red to carmine coloured shelves with a purple lustre during spawning.

Example of a prime specimen of Trout *(Salmo trutta)* weighing 12 kg.

A collection of artificial flies for salmon and trout fishing is attractive and beautiful in it self. It is not surprising that fish are not indifferent to these artificial flies and are deceived by them.

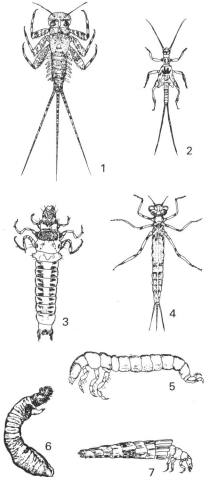

The Grayling has similar demands to the trout with regard to water purity, but unlike the latter, it can withstand slight organic pollution and higher water temperatures. The Grayling lives in shoals in open water and remains throughout the year in relatively short stretches of the river. The Grayling fry feed on tiny creatures – Protozoa, Rotatoria, aquatic crustaceans (Crustacea) – while the bigger fishes feed on the larvae of water insects – Mayfly *(Ephemeroptera)*, *Trichoptera*, *Chironomidae*, etc. In the summer season the Grayling includes in its menu dryland snails that fall onto the water surface. The Grayling has a short life-span and lives an average of 3-6 years in rivers; it is only in larger rivers and reservoirs that one might encounter 'aged' Grayling of 10-15 years but this is a rare occurrence. The growth of the Grayling depends on the expanse of water; it grows most rapidly in bigger rivers and reservoirs. When it is 5 years old it reaches a length of 300-400 mm. In rare cases individuals are caught measuring over 500 mm and weighing over 1 kg.

The Grayling reaches sexual maturity at the age of 2-3 years. It spawns from March to May at a water temperature of 7-10 °C. Spawning takes place in pairs, and the male defends the spawning site. The spawning grounds are found in flowing stretches of water with a gravel bed. There are 10,000-20,000 small eggs per 1 kg of the female's body weight. The development of the fertilized eggs lasts an average of 15 days. Artificial spawning of the Grayling and the rearing of the fry and 1 year old fish is undertaken with great success. It

Benthos – the larvae of aquatic insects in flowing waters which are the main source of food for fish particularly in the Trout and Grayling zones:
1 – the larva of the May-fly of the *Heptogenia* family, 2 – the larva of the *Plecoptera* of the *Perla* family, 3 – the larva of the *Trichoptera* of the *Limnophilus* family, 4 – the larva of the *Anisoptera* of the *Agrion* family, 5 – the larva of the *Trichoptera* of the *Polycentropus* family, 6 – the larva of *Dipterous* of the *Simulium* family, 7 – the larva of the *Trichoptera* of the *Phryganea* family.

is only thanks to artificial spawning that there is a high population of this fish and artificial breeding guarantees that the Grayling will not disappear from our waters. In view of its biological and economic qualities, the Grayling is one of the most precious fish.

The Grayling can only be fished with an artificial fly and fishing for it is justifiably regarded by anglers as the ultimate skill and the peak of the sport of angling. For many anglers who are among the admirers of these fish, 'Grayling' is a magical world which conjures up memories of tremendous experiences but also great disappointments which stimulate new resolutions as to how to win duels with this marvellous fish in the future. The duel between the Grayling and the angler is one of the most impressive confrontations in the sport of angling. In order to achieve success when fishing for Grayling, the angler must never stop learning and perfecting his skill, whilst studying the experiences of other anglers. But above all, he must know the biology of this fish and the life of the river where he is angling.

Fly-fishing – fishing with the use of artificial flies – is considered the culmination of the art of angling.

The basic prerequisite for success when fishing for Grayling is knowledge of the water as well as the ability to master the techniques of fly-fishing. Each river has its own flies that are attractive to the Grayling and if the angler is not aware of these, the result is often a great disappointment. There is no universal fly, but, in general, 20–30 flies are enough for one year's fly-fishing on most waters. It is the quest for the right fly, the testing and tying of the ideal fly that is the true magic of the sport of fly-fishing.

In the community of fish in the Grayling zone there is a mixture of species of fish from the Trout zone and Barbel zone. Together with the Brown Trout or Rainbow Trout and certain other species of fish from the Trout zone, such as the Miller's Thumb or the Minnow, the Chub and the Gudgeon or the *Aburnoides bipunctatus* can also be found.

These are typical inhabitants of the Barbel zone. And, particularly in bigger rivers, one might also encounter another inhabitant of the Barbel zone – the Huchen.

One of the most beautiful of freshwater fish –
the Grayling *(Thymallus thymallus)* is the
representative of the Grayling zone.

◄

The origins of this fish lie in the Danube and its tributaries. Today it can be found in the waters of western Germany, Austria, the Czech Republic, Poland and former Yugoslavia. The Huchen has a fusiform, cylindrical body, a wedge-shaped face, large eyes and broad, toothed jaws. Its back is greyish-brown with black spots, its sides light grey with a copper lustre and black spots, and it has a brownish belly.

This typical salmonid is very demanding with regard to water purity and oxygen content. Small specimens eat the same food as Trout, which are water insects and their larvae, whereas larger individuals only consume fish. The Huchen can live until the age of twenty or more.

It finds most of its food in the Barbel zone, where the Barbel, Nase, Chub and Gudgeon form the basis of its diet. Fishermen do not like to see the Huchen in Trout zones. Its food in these waters is the Brown Trout and also the Grayling, which is a delicacy for the Huchen. The Huchen matures at the age of four to six.

It spawns in April or May in water at a temperature of 5–10 °C. The spawning grounds are found in fairly shallow flowing waters with a gravel bed and the female fish migrate to the spawning site against the direction of the current. The female digs a bowl-shaped hole in the bed of the river, where it lays its eggs. It lays no more than about a thousand per kilo of its body weight. The fertilized eggs develop in

A fish still-life with a magnificent Grayling catch…

25–30 days. In the tributaries of the Danube, in Austria and Slovakia, the Huchen usually grows to 15–20 kilos in weight. The largest known specimen, found dead in the River Hron in 1949, weighed 49 kg and measured 210 cm.

Artificial spawning and artificial breeding are increasingly important in order to preserve the Huchen population in open waters. The Huchen is fished in the last few months of the year with a spinner or a dead fish.

In view of the size of the fish, stronger tackle is used with a firmer reel and a 0.35–0.45 mm fishing-line. Every angler dreams that one day he will catch a huge Danube Salmon.

We come across the Brook Trout in the Trout and Grayling zones of our rivers. The Brook Charr has found a suitable environment in rivers and in some valley reservoirs. ▶

Turiec – the Danubian river basin (Slovakia). A Huchen and Grayling river.

The Barbel Zone

In central stretches of rivers, where flowing waters alternate with deep pools and potholes, the river bed consists of firm gravel or sand which is stony in places and the water temperature rises to over 25°C. With the exception of the Huchen, these are no longer suitable conditions for salmonids. The fish which is typically found in these stretches of water is the Barbel, so anglers describe this area of the river as the Barbel zone. Apart from the Barbel, whose numbers have dwindled in recent years due to the damaging effects of various human activities, the other fish species characteristic of the Barbel zone are, above all, cyprinid fishes – the Nase *(Chondrostoma nasus)*, the Chub *(Leuciscus cephalus)*, the Gudgeon *(Gobio gobio)*, the *Alburnoides bipunctatus*, the omnipresent Roach *(Rutilus rutilus)* and then the Stone Loach *(Noemacheilus barbatulus)*. In larger rivers, particularly at the point where the waters flow into the Bream zone, other species appear, such as the Perch *(Perca fluviatilis)*, the Pike *(Esox lucius)* and also, in large numbers, the European Eel *(Anguilla anguilla)*.

The Common Barbel *(Barbus barbus)* is widespread in the rivers of central Europe but is not found further south, where it is replaced by other species of Barbel (e.g. *Barbus meridionalis, B. plebejus, B. peloponnensis)*. The best conditions for this species are found in central stretches of rivers. The shape of the Barbel's body, which is oval and cylindrical, but flat on the abdominal side, is ideally suited to life in the current on the river bed. Its ventral mouth on an oval head has fleshy labia passing into a kind of snout with a pair of barbels on the upper and lower lip. The eyes are relatively small and the elongated scales are firmly embedded in the skin. The overall colouring of the Barbel is brownish copper with a golden lustre. The back is olive green, the belly a yellowish to off-white colour.

The Barbel is a fish which lives in shoals close to the river bed, where it seeks out food. Its fleshy snout is capable of overturning stones, where it catches various water insect larvae concealed there *(Trichoptera, Plechoptera, Ephemeroptera)*. It devours molluscs and fibrous algae, diatoma and fine detritus. In the winter season the Barbel reduces its activity, and is the only one of the few species of the Barbel zone which waits for winter to pass in a sort of winter hibernation, hidden between stones, under leaf deposits and among roots. It is the great winter thaw waters which rouse it from its winter hibernation. The Barbel becomes extremely active prior to a storm in anticipation of the rich feast offered by the cloudy flood water which carries numerous worms, maggots and other creatures that have been swept from their shelters under stones.

The Barbel lives for many years and specimens of 25 years of age are no rarity. The females live to a greater age than the males which do not normally live more than 10 years. The females also grow more quickly than the males. The growth of the Barbel in flowing waters is relatively slow – 5 year old fish reach 200–300 mm, 10 year old ones 300–450 mm. 15 year old females measure about half a metre in length. Barbel fish of

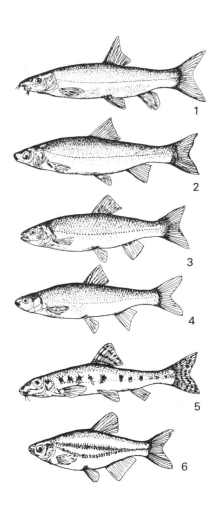

Characteristic species of fish of the Barbel zone in rivers: 1 – the Barbel *(Barbus barbus)*, 2 – the Nase *(Chondrostoma nasus)*, 3 – the Chub *(Leuciscus cephalus)*, 4 – the Dace *(Leuciscus leuciscus)*, 5 – the Gidgeon *(Gobio gobio)*, 6 – the Riffe Minnow *(Alburnoides bipunctatus)*.

A Huchen caught on a spinner. A dead fish can be used as bait.

The Trout and Grayling waters come to an end and the river gradually alters in character. The fish habitat changes simultaneously. Salmonids are replaced by the cyprinid fishes of the Barbel zone.

about 1 m in length weigh 10 kg. At present 700–850 mm fish weighing 6 kg are regarded as record specimens. The Barbel reaches sexual maturity at the age of 4–6 and reproduces from May until July. Spawning grounds are situated on the thresholds of rapids with a gravel bed. There are some 30,000–50,000 eggs per 1 kg of the body weight of the female fish, which a female spawns in some regions all at once, elsewhere in 2–3 sessions with intervals of several days between each session. The development of the embryo in a fertilized egg lasts 5–10 days, depending on the water temperature. As a result of ever worsening natural reproduction conditions, artificial reproduction of this species and the rearing of the fry up to the age of 1 to 2 has been introduced gradually. The fry are then released into rivers.

The Barbel is one of the greatest of fighters when caught by fishing tackle. The muscular body of this fish shows, at first glance, that it will not give up its life without a struggle. A Barbel weighing several kilograms can provide an angler with some agonizing moments and a successful struggle is a tremendous achievement for the angler. The Barbel bites best when the water is cloudy, usually after the floods caused by a rain storm. A medium-sized firm rod and reel is used with a bigger hook and a 0.25–0.30 mm line. The best bait when fishing with a lead weight consists of maggots, cheese or bread. Larger Barbel will bait a small fish. When fishing with a float, the larvae of water insects *(Trichoptera, Ephemeroptera,* etc.) or dung worms are used. The Barbel bites the bait energetically and the bending of the tip of the rod or the disappearance of the float are signals that the Barbel has been baited. There is immediate strong resistance once the fish is baited and the Barbel tries to escape into the current between the stones. The first assault by the Barbel usually cannot be restrained and therefore, despite the brake, the fish begins to swim away. As soon as the Barbel stops is the moment when it has to be overpowered, by gradually pulling in the line and then relaxing the hold. Resistance gradually weakens but vigilance must be maintained because even at the end of an exhausting struggle, the Bar-

The river has swollen in size, its bed is substantially broader and deeper. The water current now contains fish of the Barbel zone. ◄

bel can come to its senses and escape if one is unprepared. The catch of a heavier Barbel is always an uncompromising and exciting struggle because overpowering it is not just a matter of a couple of minutes and is certainly no mean feat.

A very significant species of the Barbel zone in most European rivers is the Nase *(Chondrostoma nasus)*. Apart from this species, further related species are found in the region of south-western Europe such as *Chondrostoma toxostoma* and *Ch. genei* in northern Italy. The Nase, originally from the Danube basin, has gradually penetrated most waters of the mainland. This silvery fish, with a slim, oval body, is dependent on flowing stretches of rivers with a firm bed where it scratches algae and *Cyanophyta* growths off stones with its ventral mouth which is specially formed for this purpose into a narrow transversal opening with angular, razor-sharp labia.

The Nase is basically a phytophagous. It swims in shoals which consist of several hundred or maybe even thousands of Nase fish. They remain in the currents, where, if one looks carefully, one can see the glistening of their bodies twisting and turning as they scratch food off stones. The Nase can adapt itself to a stagnant water environment as demonstrated by its occurrence in some valley reservoirs.

The Nase is active throughout the year in winter and summer. It is a fish that lives until middle age, up to 20 years. It grows quite slowly, 10 year old specimens measure 250–350 mm and weigh up to 1 kg. Nase weighing more than 2 kg are a rarity today. The fish reproduce for the first time at the age of 4–6 years, the female lays 3,000–6,000 eggs per kilo of her body weight. The Nase spawns in early spring with the arrival of snow waters at a temperature of 6–8 °C. It migrates to the spawning grounds often undertaking long distances against the current. Shoals of thousands

The Barbel *(Barbus barbus)* – the characteristic species of the so-called Barbel zone. If caught this fish fights for its freedom and life as few other do, and hence is a respected adversary among anglers.

59

of fish gather in stretches of water rapids. The development of the fertilized eggs depends on the water temperature and lasts 10–20 days. In the Barbel zones of the river the Nase population can be high in certain stretches, amounting to as many as 2,500 fish and 300 kg per 1 hectare of water area. In view of the fact that the Nase's natural reproduction conditions have worsened considerably, some countries (e.g. the Czech Republic) have introduced artificial spawning and rearing of fry up to 1–2 years of age. These are then released into the river.

Fishing for the Nase is very popular and there are anglers who specialize in this. It is a very delicate form of angling usually with the use of a float or sometimes with a lead weight. Delicate tackle is used with a 0.15 mm line and small hooks. Pieces of maggots, worms or even cooked rice, barley or dough can be used as bait. A so-called 'mud bait' (i.e. a small roll made of algae and lynophyta packed onto the hook) is also very successful. The angler should pull back on the line at the slightest movement of the float. Fishing for the Nase is relaxing and enjoyable, but also requires care and concentration. In the autumn months in particular the Nase has tasty, fatty flesh which is ideal for smoking processes.

The Chub *(Leuciscus cephalus)* is another significant species of the

Even such a cunning fish as the Chub was deceived and caught by a dragged spinner.

The Nase *(Chondrostoma nasus)*, which, together with the Barbel, is a typical inhabitant of the river's Barbel zone and the sought-after food of the Huchen.

Barbel zone fish community. This fish, which is adaptable enough to live in many varied waters, is usually also resistant to pollution. However, the Barbel zone of a river is its natural home. Its cylindrical, robust body begins with a relatively wide head ending in a large mouth. The body is covered with large scales. The back is blackish-green, the sides yellowy-silvery, the belly yellowish to whitish. In the Barbel zone the Chub has its own habitat in shelters. The Chub is a typical omnivore – it feeds on water insect larvae, algae, broken pieces of vegetation or the seeds, organic waste, fruit as well as fish – in other words, anything edible. It lives for up to 20 years and grows quite slowly. At 10–15 years it measures up to 500 mm and weighs about 5 kg. The largest specimens are females which live longer than the males.

The Chub spawns for the first time at 2–4 years of age. From May to June it lays its eggs in flowing waters on a gravel and sandy bed. The female spawns 50–100 thousand eggs per 1 kg of her body weight in 2 or 3 sessions. The development of the fertilized eggs lasts 3–7 days. Artificial spawning of this species is also being introduced including rearing of the fry for populating open waters. The Chub is capable of creating large populations in rivers consisting of 100–250 kg of fish per 1 hectare of water area.

Although some anglers scorn the Chub because it is an omnivore, fishing for it, and particularly catching larger specimens, is not a simple matter. The Chub knows all the tricks of the trade, and catching it should be regarded as a first-class sporting feat.

Other species of fish which are frequently found in the Barbel fish

61

The Chub *(Leuciscus cephalus)* is a much appreciated prize but catching it is no easy matter.

community include the Common Gudgeon, one of the most common fish in the Barbel zone. It grows to 15–20 cm at the age of 5–6 years. Its elongated body, resembling that of the Barbel, indicates that the Gudgeon has a similar biology and behaves in a similar way. It stays at the bottom of the river in hiding places among stones and, in favourable conditions, forms populations of large density. The Gudgeon is also found in small lowland brooks and in big rivers.

Another typical species of the Barbel zone is a small and beautiful fish – the *Alburnoides pipunctatus*. It lives to 5–6 years of age and grows as large as 15 cm in length. The fish lives in shoals and its abundant occurrence indicates that the waters which it inhabits are of good ecological quality. It is very sensitive and reacts to any deterioration in the water course. These fish which are of little interest to anglers, due to their diminutive size, are still essential to the ecological balance of the fish community.

The *Alburnoides bipunctatus* is a small fish which inhabits flowing stretches of water in shoals in the Barbel zone. Its numbers are declining due to the diminishing quality of the water.

The Dace *(Leuciscus leuciscus),* a close relative of the Chub, has a more delicate body structure and does not grow to the size of the Chub.

The Bream Zone – the Lower Course of the River

Anglers say that a true river only begins where a boat is tied up beneath an old willow tree and rocked by river waves. Every river begins as an insignificant source, brooklet and rivulet and only after a number of kilometres does it gain enough water and force to be termed a river in the true sense of the word. In its lower courses the river represents a mighty force where the water lazily rolls along the basin surrounded by meadows and forests in a broad valley. Here the water loses its ferocity, and what it picked up and swept away from the upper sections of the river basin, it now deposits in the lower course. Hence the river basin is quite shallow and the wide valley is silted up with alluvium and sediment which the river has deposited here over the course of centuries. The water course in the valley meadow often alters its basin, meandering and creating a system of river branches and islands.

The river basin cannot cope with a greater force of water, and so the flood waters overflow, transforming the entire valley meadow into one lake in which both the river and the individual branches, pools and small lakes disappear giving way to an enormous aquatic world for fishes, which, up until now, were confined to their restricted water biotopes. Once the waters subside, everything returns to its original form – the river basin directs the water currents, while water pools, small lakes and abandoned river branches re-emerge. The lower river course represents a peculiar water system where the fish fauna consists of dozens of species.

A further two fish species of Barbel waters: the Gudgeon *(Gobio gobio)* which lives close to the riverbed and the Bleak *(Alburnus alburnus)* which remains near the water surface.

The speed of the river current slows down and the Barbel zone gradually turns into the Bream zone.

The typical representative of these parts of the river is the Common Bream *(Abramis brama),* after which this section of the river is called the Bream zone.

In the Bream zone, as well as those species from the upper stretches of rivers – the Barbel, the Nase, the Chub – different species of fish appear. Most of these are related to the Common Bream, for example the *Abramis ballerus* and the Danube Bream *(Abramis sapa)* which live mainly in central and eastern parts of Europe. A further species similar

to the Bream found in abundance there is the Silver Bream *(Blicca bjo-erkna)*. The Roach *(Rutilus rutilus)* is also widespread here as well as a typical fish of lower river courses, the Orfe *(Leuciscus idus)*. Shoals of the Silver Bleak *(Alburnus alburnus)* exist here, serving as food for the sole predator among cyprinid fishes, the Asp *(Aspius aspius)*. In the Danube basin the Goldfish *(Carassius auratus)* has gradually become more widespread in the last 30 years and grows more rapidly than its relative, the Crucian Carp *(Carassius carassius)*. The Bighead Carp *(Aris-tichthys nobilis)*, which grows to a considerable size, has been appearing in recent years in the lower river courses of the Danube and Tisa

The Common Bream *(Abramis brama)*, the representative fish of the lower river's Bream zone. The Bream prefers slowly flowing or still waters.

Characteristic species of fish in the Bream zone: 1 - the Common Bream *(Abramis brama)*, 2 - the Roach *(Rutilus rutilus)*, 3 - the Orfe *(Leuciscus idus)*, 4 - the Silver Bream *(Blicca bjoerkna)*, 5 - the Perch *(Perca fluviatilis)*, 6 - the Pike *(Esox lucius)*.

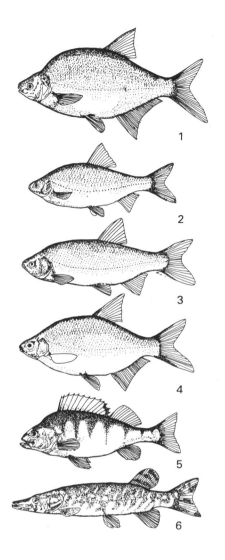

river basins. Specimens weighing 20–30 kg are caught regularly in the lower course of the rivers Morava and Ipel. This is also the home of predators – the Pike *(Esox lucius)*, the European Catfish *(Silurus glanis)*, the Pike-perch *(Stizostedion lucioperca)* and other members of the Perch *(Percidae)* family such as the Perches *(Perca fluviatilis)*, the Eastern Pike-perch *(Stizostedion volgense)*, the Ruffe *(Gymnocephalus cernua)*, the *Zingel zingel.* In the Bream zone of some water courses one sometimes encounters a species which is usually to be found in the cooler, clean waters of the Trout and Grayling zones – the Burbot. Years ago one would also encounter the Common Sturgeon *(Acipenser sturio)*, originally found in all big European rivers flowing into the nearby seas. The smallest of the Sturgeon – the Sterlet *(Acipenser ruthenus)* is found in the Danube. At the present time it is only rarely found as far up the river as Bratislava or Vienna. The biggest of the Sturgeon – the Great Sturgeon *(Huso huso)* – enters the Danube from the Black Sea. It can live up to 100 years and grows to 1 tonne in weight. However, at present, the occurrence of Sturgeon is becoming something of a legend which one hears in the stories of the oldest anglers. Yet again it was man who endangered the existence of this special fish.

The representative of this community of fishes in the Bream zone – the Common Bream *(Abramis brama)* – is an economically significant species. It is widespread in the waters of Europe north of the Alps and east of the Pyrenees. Although its original home was in the lower courses of rivers, it also found suitable living conditions in lakes, particularly valley reservoirs. It has a distinctive flat, spade-shaped body – the height is 2 to 3 times the length of the body. The head is relatively small with large eyes. The inferior mouth has a protruding snout formed to gather food from the river bed. The body is covered with large, regular scales. Younger specimens are silvery, whilst older fish acquire a darker

The Danube Bream *(Abramis sapa)* differs from the Common Bream *(Abramis brama)* in its long anal fin.

shade with a golden-yellow tinge. It lives in shoals in slow-flowing or still waters. It feeds on benthos – creatures from the river bed, particularly the larvae of the *Chironomidae*, water larvae, molluscs, *Tubificidae*, etc. Younger fishes also eat *Cladocera* and *Cyclopodea*. Detritus, particles of vegetation and grass seeds are also consumed by them.

The Bream lives for up to 10 years, but one can also find specimens which are twice that age. Its growth depends on the environment and, in particular, on the quantity of food. At 10 years it grows to 200–450 mm, but individuals of 800 mm in length weighing 6–8 kg are also found. These specimens are regarded as true Bream giants which,

The Orfe *(Leuciscus idus),* another species which prefers the river's Bream zone, is sought after by anglers.

The Perch *(Perca fluviatilis)* is also originally an inhabitant of Bream waters.

when caught, always lead to an explosion of fishing enthusiasm and increased efforts on the part of other anglers eager to acquire a similar
catch. The Bream is a typical representative of the so-called phytophile
fishes which lay their eggs on plants. The Bream spawns for the first time
at the age of 4–7 years. Spawning takes place at a temperature of 12–16°C,
whereby shoals of Bream converge on the spawning ground. This is
usually flooded meadow vegetation or aquatic vegetation where the
splashing and noisy chasing of males and females gives rise to a new generation. Some 70,000–100,000 tiny eggs are laid per 1 kg of the body
weight of a female fish. 3–4 days after fertilization the thousands of fry
hatch, of which only some reach an age to become parents.

The Common Bream is an economically significant species which is
the object of both professional and sporting anglers. It has good quality
flesh, which is tasty with a relatively high fat content. Bream meat is excellent when smoked. Many inexperienced anglers think that fishing for
Bream with a line is an easy affair, but reality proves otherwise. Bream
fishing is a real experience but also a true skill that can only be achieved
with learning and practice.

Bream generally remain at a distance from the river bank, and it is there that the angler focuses his efforts. The best procedure is to lure Bream to one place with worms, dough, cooked barley, potatoes, etc. on middle-sized hooks as bait. Fishing can be carried out with or without a float, usually with the aid of a lead weight. The Bream is very cautious and takes bait delicately, so the greatest art is knowing exactly when to pull back on the line. Although the angler might be really attentive and concentrate well, he will still miss many baits. The pulling back action must be decisive but not exaggerated, it should pass smoothly into the pull of the rod and lifting of the fish from the river bed. When overpowering the Bream, the fishing-line must be kept taut in the pull so the Bream cannot slip away. A thin rod and line can provide the angler with some memorable experiences, particularly with fish of 1–2 kg on the end of the rod. As the Bream has a very delicate mouth, it is a good idea to use a landing net to get it out of the water. Bream anglers specializing in Bream fishing form a special group of anglers, who have refined Bream fishing down to the finest details. Bream fishing is one of the greatest fishing experiences which no angler should miss.

A little known but beautiful sports fish of the Bream zone is the Orfe *(Leuciscus idus)*. It is widespread in eastern European waters. The structure of the Ide's body resembles that of its brother, the Chub, but its head and mouth are more delicate, the sides of the body are flatter and

The stake net is one of the most successful means of river fishing particularly below a weir, where fishes gather in an attempt to migrate against the current.　　▶

The *Vimba vimba,* living in the river's Barbel and Bream zone, used to be a fish found in abundance. Its numbers have considerably diminished. It is a highly prized object of angling.　　▶

it is higher. The back is greyish blue, the sides bright silver and the belly is white. A golden form of the Ide has been bred for decorative purposes. The Ide is the embodiment of agility and elegance in the lower stretches of rivers and in certain lakes. At the age of five it grows to 25–30 cm in length. It feeds on any food found in the water. The Ide reproduces in April or May and lays its eggs on a gravel or sandy bed as well as on plants and roots. Although the Ide is a flowing water fish, it can be found on the boundary, between waters with a current and a calm pool near to aquatic shrubs or bushes. Fishing for the Ide is successful with a float baited with peas or dough. Larger Ide can be caught towards the end of summer using a live fish as bait, or, even better, a Moderlieschen. It can also be baited with a spinner. However, the most successful and sought after food are insects – *Trichoptera* and *Gryllacridoidea*. The prime feeding time of the Ide is during early spring evenings, and that is the best time for anglers to go fishing. Fishing for the Ide with an artificial fly provides some truly great moments, particularly the struggle with a larger Ide specimen, which can prove fascinating and provides some instructive angling experiences.

71

The Pike is one of the fish of the Bream zone.

▼ The result of one catch in a stake net...

The misleadingly peace-loving look of the head of the Asp *(Aspius aspius)*. Nothing to hint that this is a predator and one of the *Cyprinidae* family of fish.

The Ide struggles in its own distinctive style. After being baited it starts moving quickly along the water and then heads to the bottom, when it stops, shakes its head and tries to get rid of the hook. When pulled up to the surface, it shakes and thrashes about in an effort to escape to the bottom. Ide fishing during their migration period signals the start of the fishing season and the true beginning of spring.

Rivers which are now classified as Bream zone water courses, in view of their dominant fish population, are, for the most part, quite different nowadays from their original, natural state. The water courses of most of the larger rivers have been controlled for navigation or flood protection purposes. Original lowland courses within the Bream zone were characterised by the diversity of the water environment. As well as pools of varying depths, these stretches would also have areas of shallow, flowing water interspersed with islands and rapids, many little creeks surrounded by fallen trees and extensive areas of deep water. The main body of the water course was connected with the neighbouring river floodplain via this system of various water biotopes. As a result of human intervention this naturally varied river system was replaced by monotonous canal-type troughs interrupted by weir stages and locks with lock chambers for navigation purposes. These controls meant that the low-

The Ruffe *(Acerina cernua)* lives in the lower stretches of the river, but not in great numbers.

land river was no longer characterized by a river floodplain with its alternating scenario of pools, flowing shallows, overgrown backwaters and spring floods.

The characteristic fish species of the Bream zone, such as the Common Bream, White Bream, Orfe, Pike, European Catfish and Roach, which spawn on plants, found in the natural lowland river the ideal environment and conditions for reproduction and for the fry. Therefore, there have been tremendous efforts to save the last few remaining segments of non-controlled Bream zone water courses. Likewise, in those courses which have been regulated, man is attempting to restore the diversity of the original biotopes by connecting the main streambed with a system of river dams or artificial lakes (e.g. the Rhine and Rhône rivers) outside of the confines of the controlled sluicing of the course.

The *Pelecus cultratus* lives in the Danube basin and in rivers which flow into the Baltic Sea. Its backbone is completely straight and its upward turned mouth indicates that it collects food from the surface. It has a distinctive lateral line.

The Goldfish *(Carassius auratus)* has literally invaded the waters of the Danube river basin.

All these efforts and activities are an essential contribution towards both restoring and maintaining the natural diversity of the fish population in these water courses. In those courses which are not now fragmented by human hand and where fish migration from further down the river and from the sea is still possible, the Bream zone holds many pleasant surprises for anglers. Apart from the common characteristic species mentioned above, rarer species can also be caught, such as the Sichel, Danubian Perch, Sturgeon, and also, sometimes, the Salmon or the Sea Trout, trying to reach the upper stretches of rivers where their genus used to migrate to spawn.

Industrial fishing is now being carried out on lower river courses with the use of dragnets. A net being hauled on the banks of the Danube.

It is the great diversity of the fish stock of the Bream zone and the potentially rare catches, which makes the fishing so attractive in these waters.

A detailed view of the head of the Sterlet *(Acipenser ruthenus)*, which lives in the Danube basin.

The Carp *(Cyprinus carpio)* is the original inhabitant of the lower courses of big rivers. The photo shows an original wild river Carp which has a cylindrical body and differs considerably from the forms of domesticated carp found in fishponds. ▶

Pools, Small Lakes and Abandoned River Branches

In the areas surrounding smaller water biotopes one comes across remains from the time when the river annually flooded its banks and its waters flooded the surrounding countryside, or the remains of the original riverbed left behind when the river diverted into a new basin. The abandoned branches, pools and smaller lakes are left without permanent contact with the water course that contributed towards their origin.

In the lower regions of large river courses, when the waters swell, they often flood an extensive surrounding territory – so-called inundated territory – so that an entire river course of pools, abandoned river branches and small lakes is joined together into one large lake. Scattered island trees and shrubs protrude from the extensive water plain of flooded territory where optimum conditions arise for fish-breeding and feeding. ▶

Angling on lower courses of big rivers has a particular charm similar to being at the sea.
◄

There are only exceptional cases when the flood waters of some rivers annually merge their small water biotopes with their main river basin and become one large lake, when the great waters flood the surrounding, so-called inundated territory. These small water biotopes represent a specific water world where certain species of fish, originally from the Bream zone of bigger rivers, find suitable living conditions. Pools and old river branches, after losing contact with the mother course, disappear little by little over a number of years, as they are gradually silted up and overgrown with aquatic plants. Most of these waters are typical for their lush growth of aquatic plants. Most pools, old river shoulders and small lakes are surrounded by an area of bushes, willows, sallows and alders. High marsh plants, such as reeds *(Phragmites communis), Glyceria aquatica,* Saprganium, yellow Iris, Acorus and reed-mace *(Typhaceae)* are found on the edges. In summer, the water surface becomes a carpet of beautiful water-lilies, particularly Batrachium. Below the water surface there are cabbage roses and elodei. This rich occurrence of plants in the pools and their surrounding area secures a rich input of organic matter which decays to form an enormous layer of mud on the bottom.

A situation could occur, particularly in the winter, when the decay of organic matter and plants underneath the ice drains all the oxygen from the water causing the fish to die. If these waters are not permanently or partly in contact with a river, the only fish which can survive there are those which are capable of living in water with a low oxygen content. The Tench *(Tinca tinca)* and the Crucian Carp *(Carassius carassius)* are such fish which survive even in circumstances when the content of the dissolved oxygen comes close to a zero value. The Rudd *(Scardinius erythrophthalmus)* also finds a suitable environment in pools and old river shoulders.

Two anglers working together in the final stage of a struggle with a fish in a pool on the inundated territory of the River Dyje. ▶

The abandoned river branches and pools which have lost their permanent link with the mother course of the river, create a specific water environment. The fish found here are those which do well in stagnant water, such as the Common Bream *(Abramis brama)* and the Roach *(Rutilus rutilus)*. The Tench *(Tinca tinca)* is one such fish which thrives best in the stagnant waters of the inundated territory of lower river courses.

The Grass Carp *(Ctenophyryngodon idella)*, imported to Europe from eastern Asia (the Amur river basin), has found suitable conditions in overgrown pools and river branches, as indicated by the catch shown in this picture.
◄

The Rudd is an excellent sports fish, and is one of only a few fish which feed on parts of soft aquatic plants. One also encounters other fishes here from the Bream zone of rivers, such as the Common Bream, the Silver Bream, the Roach, the Perch, the Pike, the European Catfish and the Carp.

The Tench *(Tinca tinca)* is found throughout Europe with the exception of northern Scandinavia and some extreme parts of southern Europe. It originally lived in the lower stretches of bigger rivers where it found the most suitable conditions in inundated pools, lakes and abandoned river branches. The Tench and the Carp are reared in fishponds. The Tench's relatively short, robust body with a proportionately sized head and small eyes is covered in tiny scales deeply embedded in the skin. The surface of the skin has a strong slimy layer so that the Tench is very slimy and slippery, similar to the Eel for example. The basic colouring of the Tench is greenish brown with a copper to golden lustre. The most suitable environment for the Tench is in eutrophic and overgrown marsh waters with a low content of dissolved oxygen. The Tench is a thermophilic fish and when the water temperature drops under 5°C it falls into a latent state in winter (hibernation). Its main food are benthic creatures which it skilfully removes from the muddy bed and also detritus.

The Tench is a fish of average growth. The best size for consumption is 200–400 g which it reaches at the age of 3–5 years. Giant-sized Tench can measure up to 600 mm in length and weigh 4–5 kg. It reaches sexual maturity at the age of 3–4 years and spawns during June and July in

The Tench *(Tinca tinca)*: the stagnant water area (pools and river branches) of downstream inundated territories is its preferred environment.
▶

2–3 sessions. It lays the eggs on plants and their development lasts 3–5 days. It is highly fertile with 150,000–200,000 eggs per kilo of the female's body weight. In recent years artificial spawning of the Tench has been introduced and there are efforts to increase its breeding in fishponds.

The Tench has very tasty flesh, which is particularly appreciated in Austria, Italy and Germany. Tench meat is delicate and is similar in structure to that of salmonids but with a higher content of fat. Fishing for the Tench with a line is no simple matter. The Tench is a very careful fish and its numbers in pools and similar waters are far higher than one would guess judging by the few catches made by anglers. The best place to find Tench is near water vegetation or in open spaces within it. The Tench bites best in May and June and then at the end of August, during other months the best baiting opportunities for Tench are in the early morning or early evening on a warm, calm day. Various worms – dung worms or maggots – dough, potatoes, barley or dumplings can be used as bait. Anglers often achieve unexpected success if they use the larvae of *Trichoptera* and *Plecoptera* as bait.

In the Danube and Dniester river basins, particularly in inundated regions and in the Hungarian Lowland in canals with clean water, there lives a small rare fish whose existence is seriously threatened by irrigation and drainage work. This fish is the Mudminnow *(Umbra krameri)*.

Anglers fish for Tench in overgrown waters, usually using a small float with the bait just above the river bed. The Tench bites gently and appears to be playing with the bait. The float indicates this because when the Tench begins to bite, it jerks and rocks about on the water, disappears and resurfaces or moves round in small circles. Anglers should exert considerable force after the float has been drawn down 2–3 m. Once the Tench has been hooked, it should be pulled up to the surface and out of the water as quickly as possible so it does not become entangled in the growth of aquatic plants or other obstacles.

The Weatherfish *(Misgurnus fossilis)* is an inhabitant of marshy areas where it can withstand oxygen free waters. It is an unknown fish to many anglers who don't often find it in their landing net.

A first sight one has the impression that the Pumpkinseed *(Lepomis gibbosus)* comes from foreign waters and that European waters are not its home. It was imported into Europe from North America in the last century and one can come across it in several European waters. It has found suitable living conditions in pools, abandoned river branches and small lakes near rivers.

A Golden Tench catch is always cheering for an angler, even though the fish does not grow to a great size. There is still a great deal of debate with regard to Tench fishing and this subject opens up a broad field of knowledge still to be acquired.

In warmer regions the trial introduction has begun of a fish which was imported into Europe from the Far East – the Grass Carp *(Ctenopharyngodon idella)*. The Grass Carp feeds mainly on aquatic plants and therefore is well utilized in overgrown pools and river lakes, where it contributes towards the restriction of undesirable aquatic plants of which there is usually an unsustainable amount. The first experiences of Grass Carp in the open waters of Germany, Hungary and former Czechoslovakia or Rumania show that this species may prove beneficial to anglers. The Grass Carp does not reproduce naturally in Europe so its numbers are determined by the amount of fry acquired from artificial spawning and breeding. It grows quite well and reaches 20–30 kg in weight. As far as food is concerned, it is classed as an omnivore which feeds primarily on aquatic plants. At first sight it resembles the Chub, and its stocky and muscular body indicates that it is a fighter fish. When caught on a line it struggles more than most other fish, so overpowering a larger specimen is a case of equal combat. If the angler wins this struggle it

85

is considered an admirable feat. A strong rod is used when fishing for Grass Carp together with a stronger line and a bigger reel. These specially strengthened aids are required to overpower a 10 kilo fish. When Grass Carp devour aquatic plants, it appears as though a mysterious force is at work. A growth of reed-mace standing at the edge of a pool suddenly begins to shake, then it bends over and is dragged off along the water surface and gradually disappears into the digestive tract of the herbivorous Grass Carp.

Angling in water pools, branches and small lakes in the area surrounding a big river opens an attractive and mysterious world of silence far removed from the rest of the world. Therefore many anglers seek out a pool, small lake or abandoned river branch when the new angling season begins. There hidden somewhere in the broad meadows or meadowland forests awaits a mysterious kingdom. Always changing in every season of the year, and therefore so attractive that not even a swarm of bloodthirsty gnats can discourage the true angler from his goal.

Some English rivers differ in the character of their surrounding area from similar rivers on the Continent.

Will the Salmon Survive until the Year 2000?

The entrance gate from the sea to freshwater river systems is formed by the mouth of rivers. For the Atlantic Salmon this is where the journey begins to the spawning grounds in the upper stretches of the river and this is the route back taken by those individuals that survive after spawning. It is here that the young Salmon swim into the sea to mature and, as adults, return to their birthplace to produce the next generation of their species.

In the past the Salmon *(Salmo salar)* was a species generally found in European rivers flowing into the North Sea and the Atlantic Ocean, with the exception of the Iberian Peninsula. However, the question now being asked is: Will the Salmon survive until the year 2000? In a number of countries where there are still surviving eye-witnesses, an abundant occurrence of the Salmon is a thing of the past. For example, at the beginning of this century the Salmon could still be found in the rivers Elbe, Rhine, Thames and throughout Denmark. It is now on the decline in Poland and the Baltic Sea coast. In his construction of water levels that are insurmountable for the Salmon in their journey against the current,

his extensive water pollution and his introduction of mass fishing in fresh waters and seas, man is endangering the existence of this species of the European freshwater ichthyofauna. In order to understand the current problems of this species, one has to understand the biology and way of life of the Salmon.

The Salmon is a typical representative of the group called salmonids. It is one of the only several species which live in fresh waters (rivers) and in seas. It makes its long journey between these two water systems during the course of its life at various stages of development in order to fulfil its life's mission – the preservation of its species. After reaching sexual maturity, the Salmon heads for its native river to lay the foundations

The Shannon, a typical salmon river in Ireland. It is here that the Salmon and other fish species such as the Sea Trout *(Salmo trutta trutta)* and the European Eel *(Anguilla anguilla)* undertake so-called anadramous migration. ▶

Various waterworks have made it impossible
for the Salmon to make the journey to their
spawning ground under natural conditions, so
man has created artificial water routes for
them – fish crossings or 'steps' to enable them
to overcome these obstacles.

◀

of a new generation. The migration to spawning grounds vary in distance, from several dozen kilometres (e.g. along short rivers in the British Isles) to hundreds of kilometres (e.g. along the rivers Elbe, Vistula, Rhine). Salmon spawn from October until December, usually upstream where the best environment exists for the development of fertilized eggs. The female hollows out a 'nest' (redd) in the gravel river bed where it covers the spawned eggs with the same material. After spawning, the mother fish usually return to the sea, and during the journey many of them perish or are caught by anglers. In spring (April, May) young Salmon known as 'alevins' hatch from the fertilized eggs and they remain at their birth site for 2–3 years until they reach about 20 cm in length. The young Salmon fishes are called 'smolt' and, when they have grown to the appropriate size they head for the sea. There, in 2–3 years, they grow to

For most European anglers a Salmon catch *(Salmon calar)* only is a dream, which would involve a long journey along rivers in Scandinavia or the British Isles.

A detailed view of the head of a Salmon radiates the 'nobility' of this fish.

adulthood, and as fishes of 6–10 kg reach sexual maturity and return to their birthplace to spawn. Some males remain in the river after spawning and take part in further spawning rather than returning to the sea. Only a small number of fish return to the river twice or, exceptionally, three times to spawn. They live a hard life, with many extra sufferings now inflicted by man.

In northern and western Europe, where the Salmon has hitherto been an economically significant species, efforts are being made to protect and maintain the large numbers of this species. At water works (dam walls, high weirs on water courses) which prevent Salmon from migrating to the spawning grounds, 'fish crossings' are being built to enable fishes heading upstream to overcome obstacles and reach spawning grounds located at a higher level of the river. In north European countries artificial Salmon breeding has been introduced, whereby eggs are artificially spawned, hatched in hatcheries and the reared smolts are released into the river. Salmon protection has also been implemented in the form of restriction of sea fishing and the protection of females when fishing in rivers.

Fishing for Salmon with a line is very attractive even though anglers usually have to travel far to catch the fish. The most important Salmon rivers are now for the most part found in Norway, Sweden and the British Isles. The most successful Salmon fishing season is at the start of their journey to the spawning grounds, which varies from river to river during the period from April to June. The most successful Salmon fishing grounds are such rivers where, after a short stretch, the river is

A Salmon catch by professional anglers in dragnets. Despite the constantly declining catches, salmon fishing is still popular, because of the attractive prices which it fetches.

interrupted by an unsurmountable obstacle (rapids, weir, dam wall) which hinders them in continuing their journey upstream. Usually most catches are made at the beginning of the Salmon migration, when they have not yet lost the great appetite for food that they were used to in the sea. Salmon fishing requires special tackle, because heavy fish catches are quite common. Anglers usually fish for Salmon with artificial baits – big artificial Salmon flies and spinners. One should be equipped with tackle for Salmon fishing with a line and for fly-fishing, because their appetite for bait tends to vary. The technique for Salmon fishing with an artificial fly and line is similar to that of fishing for other salmonids. Salmon baiting, the struggle with the fish and the catch is an experience for which central European anglers now travel a long way.

In view of the high prices which they attract, Salmon are a sought after object for fishing by professional anglers in rivers and on the open sea. Intensive sea fishing poses a particularly serious danger for the continuing existence of this species, because fish caught in the sea are those that still have not had a chance to spawn. Fishing statistics show that the increase in Salmon catches on the open sea is accompanied by a decline in the number of individual fish heading for rivers to spawn. Efforts are being made to restrict fishing for immature Salmon. Therefore the feeding of these fish in net cages situated in sea fjords and sea lochs is on the increase.

The struggle to preserve the Salmon, a species which could become unknown to future generations, has gradually begun on a wide scale, although not all of the relevant countries are contributing to or participating in these endeavours.

The European Eel

The European Eel *(Anguilla anguilla)* is one of those species of fish whose life depends on both a sea and freshwater environment. Since time immemorial the Eel has been one of those creatures whose life was unknown and mysterious. The reproduction of the Eel, in particular, opened up the gates of human imagination. Ancient intellectuals, including Aristotle, believed that freshwater Eel had no sexual organs and were born in the depths of the sea or hatched from the steam and mist above the water. It was not until the 19th century that the conjectures about the reproduction of this species were laid to rest, when it was proved that the Eel spawns in the sea depths far from inland waters. At the youngest stage of its development, it journeys to the coastal and river courses right up to inland waters. Despite the fact that knowledge about this species is more or less complete, the Eel, in the minds of anglers, is one of the most mysterious of fish whose biology is surrounded by all sorts of conjecture.

It is the European Eel species *(Anguilla anguilla)* that is found in European waters. What is the course of a European Eel's life? Adult Eels leave fresh water – lakes and rivers – and journey to the sea. After reaching sea waters, their journey to the reproduction site begins. The spawning grounds of the European Eel are the sea depths of the Sargasso Sea in the subtropical part of the Atlantic ocean marked roughly by the

Some old sluice-gates in a river provide shelter for many fish including eels.

25-27°C northern latitude and the 52-65°C western longitude. Here, where the depth of sea extends to about 6,000 m, the spawning of the Eel takes place in the spring months at 150-600 m beneath the surface. The mother fish that have given rise to a new generation of the species, die after spawning. About 5 mm tiny glassy, transparent larvae shaped like willow leaves with large teeth (which were originally described as a separate species - *Leptocephalus brevirostris)* hatch from the fertilized eggs. From their birth place, the Eel larvae are either passively carried along or actively move towards the coasts of Europe. Their journey lasts 2.5-3 years, and when they reach the shelf waters near the European mainland they measure about 80 mm. It is there that their metamorphosis takes place and they take on the eel form (Glass Eel). The

93

The newly-hatched Eel larvae are caught at the mouth of rivers flowing into the sea, then transported inland and freed into river basins upstream. So man enables the Eel to reach its first journey's destination seeing as it is man's activities (waterworks, pollution) which have closed off the waterways for the Eel.

small eels, sometimes called the 'montée', appear at the mouths of rivers and journey inland against the current.

By constructing various steps (levels) and dams, and by causing water pollution in rivers further downstream, man has, in many cases, made migration of the Eel montée into inland freshwaters impossible. In

A catch of mysterious fish – the European Eel – its body resembling the body of a snake. The European Eel *(Anguilla anguilla)* makes a tempting catch for every angler.

view of the fact that the Eel is an economically significant species, efforts are being made to enable it to reach these inland waters. On a number of steps special fish crossings have been constructed for small eels. In Great Britain special 'mini-crossings' for eels have been constructed in the shape of gutters forming an artificial S-shaped water course with a slow-flowing water flow via which small eels can surmount a weir or dam and reach the river basin. Where pollution of water courses has made the further journey from the sea impossible, the 'glass eels' are caught, transported inland and released into lakes, reservoirs, fishponds and water courses.

The small eels, after reaching their new home in fresh water, begin their, on average, one decade stage of life. The Eel has an unusual, snake-like body covered in slimy, strong skin interwoven with a system of blood capillary vessels. Tiny scales appear on the skin of the older fishes. Apart from its protective function, the skin contributes towards supplying the Eel's body with oxygen and, together with the swim-bladder which is connected by a passage to the gullet, it complements the breathing function of the gills. In many European countries specific eel breeding farms have been built equipped with water throughout the year and intensive feeding. Many of these farms acquire Eels for further breeding in Great Britain.

During the period of its life in fresh water, the Eel is a typical individualistic fish which lives on the river-bed (benthonic) concealed in shelters and, unless it is afflicted by the migratory instinct, it stays in one habitat. It is active in its movements and usually seeks out food at night or in cloudy water, with some exceptions. It spends the winter season in a latent winter hibernation and is at its most active from May till September. It belongs to the so-called euryhalinic species which has

Eels caught during the night in an eel catcher – a fish-sluice. This is a special type of trapping device for catching eels on their journey back to the sea. The water current falls through the lattice-work catching basin and the trapped eel slides along the slanted area of the grated bottom into the trap-box. From here the catch is collected daily using the fish-sluice.

no problem surviving in water of various salt concentrations. The main food of the Eel in fresh waters are benthonic invertebrates, the so-called benthos, such as water insect larvae, molluscs, small fishes, water worms, etc. The Eel poses a great threat to all species of crab

The remains of a tree – the stump with its roots is used as a reinforcement for preventing the water current from expanding its power to this piece of the riverbank.

◄

whose numbers the Eel can virtually eradicate, particularly in enclosed reservoirs.

The female Eel stays in fresh water for 8–12 years growing to at least 60 cm or more in length. Then it begins the so-called catadromous migration back to the sea. The males, which grow at a much slower rate, begin to migrate back to the sea at 6–9 years of age when they measure up to 40 cm. The migration of eels along the direction of the current is most intensive during the season of higher water flow. In that season eels develop a silvery colouring, their eyes become enlarged and further changes occur to the skin which gains in strength. After reaching the sea, the eels head for the spawning site on a journey that lasts 1.5 to 2 years at a speed of 40–50 km a day.

The meat of the Eel contains 20–30 % fat. It is therefore tasty when smoked. In the subconscious of the angler the Eel is still enveloped in mystery and therefore, for most anglers, catching it by line is very attractive. What is decisive for a successful Eel catch is the right selection of the site for angling. Usually these are deeper waters with adequate shelter, such as stones, stone dikes, embankments, hollowed out banks with roots of trees, leaves, shrubs and brushwood. The Eel goes foraging for food at dusk and night, so this is the best time for a successful catch. Fishing is carried out with a zinc weight at the bottom with a strong line and harder rod. The bait consists of either worms, or a small live or dead fish. The Eel usually takes the bait itself, but one has to wait patiently. Once it takes the bait and when pulling back on the line, it feels like the hook has been driven into an inanimate object followed by snake-like twisting. The rule is to lift the baited eel energetically from the bottom and out of the water as quickly as possible because any hesitancy will allow the eel time to swim to shelter and escape. Every angler catching an eel has his own often comical and unbelievable experiences. The Eel can 'disappear' from an airtight enclosed holding net or an undisturbed sack, all it needs is a tiny hole to slip out and escape back into the water. The endeavours of inexperienced anglers to take hold of a caught eel are similar to the entertainment of silent comedies.

The Eel is caught by professional anglers in special net traps situated alongside river banks and lakes. Eel traps in the form of fish sluices strain the water current successfully, catching eels which migrate in the direction of the current downstream towards the sea to spawn. Many eels perish when passing through the turbines of hydro-electric power plants as they do not have any repelling device when they are trying to migrate back to the sea. Polluted stretches of rivers also often represent an impervious barrier for eels heading towards the sea.

VALLEY RESERVOIRS

Natural water biotopes arise and evolve for a long period of time spanning that of many human lives. On the contrary, within only a few years and as a result of the work of skilled human hands assisted by machinery, a dammed valley reservoir, often of enormous dimensions, can appear. Man is literally changing the landscape day by day and creating a new water environment which provides fish with very favourable conditions. Human society usually has a negative effect on water systems, but in the case of valley reservoirs, it is creating new water worlds which are a significant and positive contribution as far as fish are concerned.

Valley reservoirs appear after the damming of a river valley with a barrier made of concrete or heaped natural materials. The lake above the dam barrier then fills up with water. The resulting lake floods and covers up both the stretch of the river and the actual valley with its fields, meadows and forests as well as human settlements, roads and other structures. The size and extent of valley reservoirs vary from several dozen to thousands of hectares or even thousands of square kilometres. Under European conditions, whereby the landscape is densely populated, the water area of valley reservoirs only rarely exceeds a thousand hectares. Valley reservoirs are important not only for energy and water management but also for fishing. They provide fish with suitable conditions for survival and fishing in these water biotopes has become very important and widespread despite the short time that this has been available – its development only began in the 20th century.

With regard to fish and fish habitats, the valley reservoir represents a great experiment carried out in nature where we can observe the changes which occur. The original fast running river current where a certain ichthyofauna was formed over a long period, in a short space of time has changed into an extensive, stagnant stretch of water with totally different properties and conditions. The flood waters of a reservoir signify an ecological catastrophe for the original inhabitants of the reservoir area, as most of these species either perish or disappear, giving way to the formation of an entirely new population. This forms gradually, creating and inhabiting a new water ecosystem that is very different to the original. What are the sources of the

The moods of a lake.

99

new fish families in a recently created valley reservoir? Well, of the original fish population of the flooded stretch of river and other water courses in the flooding area, only those species which are adaptable to the new environment will survive there, as indeed will those who find the new environment more suitable than the previous one. A further source for the creation of a fish colony in the new reservoir is its water basin where species are found which, in various ways – by tributaries – get to the reservoir and if they find suitable conditions there then they settle down. A significant source for new species of fish being introduced to a valley reservoir is man who, whether intentionally or at random, releases fish into the reservoir.

When fishing at valley reservoirs a boat is used both on the water and sometimes at the bank. Will it be this cast that will bring success? The thought must cross the mind of every angler.

The Pike – the wide-open toothed jaws are typical of this predator of the water kingdom – who is the goal of every angler's catch. It is valley reservoirs that conceal pike of breathtaking size in their watery depths.

A number of stumps – tree 'monuments' – for which the valley reservoir meant the end of life. ▶

A view of a dam lake stirs up peculiar feelings when one remembers the original river valley which has disappeared beneath the water surface forever. ▶▶

101

The formation and development of a fish colony in a new valley reservoir lasts a number of years before a relatively permanent state is created.

The development of a fish colony in a new valley reservoir can be divided into three stages: the commencement stage, the transitional stage and the stage of stability. The commencement stage usually lasts 3–6 years, which is typical for the change in character of the water environment from flowing (lotic) water to stagnant (lenitive) water. An extensive area of the river valley is flooded – fields, meadows or felled trees, whereby dry land organisms have declined, leading to the gradual extraction of nutrients from the region of the new valley reservoir. As a result, in this first stage, there is a strong development of plankton organisms, particularly zooplankton and benthonic water organisms. As a consequence of the changes in the character of the water environment suitable conditions arise above all for those species of fish suited to slow flowing water (limnophilic) and for highly adaptable species. Current-loving (reophilic) species, originally predominant in the rivers, decline and disappear. In the first few years conditions in the valley reservoirs are ideal for the reproduction of fish species which spawn on plant substrata (phytophilic species) and indifferent species which spawn on any kind of base according to the conditions. Therefore such fish as the Pike *(Esox lucius)*, the Roach *(Rutilus rutilus)*, the Common Bream *(Abramis brama)* and the Perch *(Perca fluviatilis)* set up colonies at the beginning of this first stage. What is also typical of the commencement stage in the development of ichthyofauna in the reservoir is the rapid growth of all species, because there is a large amount of food available.

In the subsequent transitional stage the nutrient content in the reservoir declines, the amount of food decreases and the conditions get worse for the reproduction of Phytophilic species of fish. The breeding and production capacity of the reservoir is saturated and gradually the species which are suited to this environment establish a presence there. Reophilic species (e.g. the Nase, Barbel, Chub, etc.) of fish disappear, unless they adapt to the environment of the reservoir. Species which in the first stage of the existence of the reservoir, have undergone some sort of population explosion, e.g. the Pike, Perch, Roach, gradually stabilize their numbers at a certain level. The reservoir's fauna becomes more firmly established.

After roughly 10–15 years, most valley reservoirs reach a stage of stability when conditions in the reservoir are balanced, so that the water system acquires a regular rhythm. Chemical conditions also become stabilized and the relations and functions begin to work between the individual sections of the ecosystem of the reservoir as one whole. Basically a stable fish colony in the reservoir is created, and any further changes take place much more slowly.

As far as the species composition of the reservoir's ichthyofauna is concerned, there are distinct salmonid and cyprinid reservoirs. Valley reservoirs with salmonid type fish colonies are found at greater heights above sea level on courses of the Trout zone, where the water temperature reaches a maximum of 15–20°C. The nutrition of these waters is relatively low. These are usually reservoirs of a valley basin type with fairly deep water. The basis of the fish colony is formed by the Trout, which takes on a lake form here *(Salmo trutta morpha*

lacustris), accompanied by the Charr *(Salvelinus arcticus).* In some reservoirs, particularly new ones, the Rainbow Trout *(Salmo gairdneri)* makes a distinctive appearance in the first few years when there is sufficient zooplankton present. In valley reservoirs where there are acid waters with low pH (4–5) values, the Brook Trout *(Salvelinus fontinalis)* has a good chance of thriving. In some smaller valley reservoirs even the Grayling *(Thymallus thymallus)* adapts to the conditions of slow flowing or still waters, usually living longer and growing to a greater size (1.0–2.5 kg). Also the freshwater Salmon – Huchen *(Hucho hucho)* finds suitable conditions in some valley reservoirs thereby attracting the interest of anglers, as it can grow to the trophy size of up to 30 kg in this environment. Whitefishes *(Coregonidae),* originally lake fishes, also find the conditions favourable in some

The extensive water surface of the valley reservoir lake attracts anglers like a magnet.

The Brown Trout exists in a lake form in valley reservoirs. A prime catch a coloured beauty which has unwillingly been taken from its watery world to make a lucky angler happy.

valley reservoirs. The salmonid character of fish colonies in valley reservoirs is maintained because the conditions there (e.g. temperature) do not suit other fish species such as the Pike, Perch or cyprinid fishes.

The species spectrum of the fish colony in valley reservoirs of a cyprinid character is more varied and multifarious. These reservoirs contain warm water which rises to 20–30°C in the summer season. The water contains many more nutrients and, particularly in shallow stretches, is rich in growth of taller aquatic plants. These reservoirs are situated at a lower level than those of salmonid character and are

The Perch *(Perca fluviatilis)* and the Pike *(Esox lucius),* two different species, characteristic of most valley reservoirs and the same greedy predators.

often exclusively of a lowland lake type. The leading fish species, which also form the most significant element of the fish colony, are members of the cyprinid *(Cyprinidae)* family and particularly limnophilic species – the Roach *(Rutilus rutilus)*, the Common Bream *(Abramis brama)*, the Silver Bream *(Blica bjoerkna)*, the Bleak *(Alburnus alburnus)*, in some also the Carp *(Cyprinus carpio)*, the Tench *(Tinca tinca)* and others. Of the other groups, amongst the most significant species are the Pike *(Esox lucius)* and Pike-perch *(Stizostedion lucioperca)* which are considered the fish gems of most valley reservoirs, and are of tremendous interest to anglers in central Europe. In most valley reservoirs one of the most important fish is also the Perch *(Perca fluviatilis)*. One can continue to count the numerous fish species found in valley reservoirs – the Rudd *(Scardinius erythrophthalmus)*, the Goldfish *(Carassius carassius)*, the Asp *(Aspius aspius)*, the Ruffe *(Gymnocephalus cernua)*, the European Eel *(Anguilla anguilla)*, etc.

Every valley reservoir is unique, possessing its own individual properties and conditions. Therefore the fish colony of each reservoir, apart from its characteristic elements, also differs in species of fish, as well as in the numbers of the typical species. Hence fishing also differs from one valley reservoir to the next. It is full of surprises, whether in the catch of unexpected species or in the number of prime specimens caught.

Important food organisms for fishes in still waters: 1 – *Cladocera* of the *Daphnia* family, 2 – *Cladocera* of the *Ceriodaphnia* family, 3 – *Cyclopoidea* of the *Cyclops* family, 4 – *Cyclopoidea* of the *Diaptomus* family, 5 – the *Branchiopus* family, 6 – the larva of the gnat of the *Culex* family, 7 – the larva of the *Chironomidae* of the *Chironomus* family.

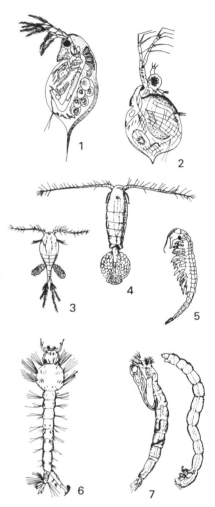

The Pike-perch *(Stizostedion lucioperca)*, an original species of larger water courses, has found very favourable living conditions in valley reservoirs particularly in view of their clean water.

A 'prime' Pike-perch in the meshes of a net used by professional anglers for fishing and by researchers during ichthyologic studies of fish habitats in valley reservoirs. The mesh net is one of the most highly effective fishing nets.

There are some generally binding rules for fishing of valley reservoirs. Every angler gradually adds to the rules and improves his technique after gaining his own experience and knowledge. The fishing tackle must be suitable and in perfect condition to ensure that a prime fish does not escape from a weak line and disappear in the watery depths. Likewise on an extensive water surface a larger and stronger rod and reel are required as the line has to be cast further from the bank. It is advisable to have several types of rods if fishing for several days, so that the method of angling can be changed as necessary. The anglers who have an advantage when fishing a valley reservoir are those who knew the river valley before it was flooded. Local ex-

perts know the various depths, they even know the bottom and places where there are faults which can make fishing most unpleasant. Knowledge of a reservoir provides anglers with a far greater chance of success than fishing at an unknown reservoir for the first time. Those who are unfamiliar with a reservoir should seek advice from friends or locals if possible. Information gained from angling colleagues who know the water can simplify fishing considerably. A boat, particularly on larger lakes, makes fishing much easier and allows anglers to move to different fishing sites quickly. Fishing from a boat on a valley reservoir makes it possible to fish at sites which are inaccessible from the bank and where there is often a good chance of a prime fish catch. Fishing at valley reservoirs is becoming increasingly attractive for most anglers.

Fish in valley reservoirs grow to a greater size than those in flowing waters, and the chance of catching giants - ageing fish - spurs on many an angler. Valley reservoirs really are becoming a fishing paradise. It is in these reservoirs that anglers have achieved a number of catches of European or world standard.

Valley reservoirs have become the perfect environment for another species of fish, attractive to anglers because of its unpredictability and the uncertainty as to whether it can be caught. Every real angler

The final stage of overpowering a Pike-perch. A hook is used instead of a landing-net with bigger catches.

The fight is won – a lovely Pike-perch catch.

knows that the fish in question is the beauty of the *Percidae* family, the Pike-perch. This species has become a typical inhabitant of most valley reservoirs.

The Pike-perch *(Stizostedion lucioperca)* is widespread in the waters of central and eastern Europe right up to the River Elbe basin.

It has been artificially reared and released into waters further west. It is not found, however, in the waters of Italy, the Balkans, northern parts of Scandinavia and in certain parts of the British Isles. Originally it was a fish of valley rivers but it was soon introduced to fishponds. Valley reservoirs have provided the Pike-perch with very favourable conditions so it is now a symbolic fish of these artificially created water lakes. One encounters the Pike-perch in most still waters such as pools, lakes, abandoned river branches and lakes formed after gravel and sand mining as well as forgotten valley reservoirs. This fish does best in extensive waters with a sand-clay bed and requires relatively clean water with sufficient oxygen content. The Pike-perch has an oblong, relatively stocky, fusiform body with a wedge-shaped head. It has big, glassy eyes, a terminal toothed mouth with two large 'dog' like teeth at the end of the lower jaw. The body is covered with

Industrial fishing in valley reservoirs can also be carried out using a drag-net measuring up to 300 m in length. After closing up both ends of the drag-net, the final stage of dragging the net onto the bank begins. ▶

110

Wooded slopes of the original river valley now envelop the pearl-like valley reservoir lake whose depths offer favourable conditions for fish fauna.

◄

coarse ctenoid scales. The basic colouring of the Pike-perch is grey-ish-green with blackish-brown stripes on the sides fading to spots, while the belly is white. The smaller brother of the Pike-perch, the Eastern Pike-perch *(Stizostedion volgensis)* is found in the tributaries of the Black Sea and the Caspian Sea.

The Pike-perch is a typical predator and, with the exception of the smallest fishes which feed mainly on zooplankton and benthos, the

Pike-perch eats fish of substantial size. Even Pike-perch of 30–40 mm in size ferociously attack and devour embryos of fish only slightly smaller than themselves, such as the Carp and Roach as well as the Perch and other species. The Pike-perch lives in small shoals and even the largest Pike-perch lives in smaller groups. In contrast to the Pike, the Pike-perch does not stay close to the bank, and tends to remain deep down in the water. On average it lives for 8–12 years. If it has sufficient food, it grows relatively quickly. It can reach 990–1,300 mm in length and weigh up to 10–20 kg at the extremely old age of about 20 years.

The Pike-perch attains sexual maturity at 3–5 years and spawns from April to June at a water temperature of 8–14°C. The male prepares a sort of spawning nest with a diameter of 50–100 cm using roots and twigs or sand for the base on which the eggs are laid. After the eggs have been spawned, the male guards the nest and disperses slime and dirt with its fins. The Pike-perch has relatively small eggs and the female usually lays about 100,000–120,000 eggs per 1 kg of her body weight. The eggs develop in 20–30 days depending on the water temperature. Pike-perch reproduction is also carried out semi-artificially. The mother fish spawn in prepared nests made of willow and bent-grass roots. The spawned eggs are then reared and the embryo or older fry are used for populating open waters.

The Pike-perch is one of the most precious of fish in our fresh waters and it is of considerable economic importance in a number of water courses. It is of high consumer value and its meat is of the same high quality as many sea fish. Hence, many anglers concentrate on Pike-perch fishing, despite the Pike-perch being considered a re-

A catch using a drag-net mainly contains the most abundant species – i.e. the Common Bream *(Abramis brama)*, the Roach *(Rutilus rutilus)* and even the Perch *(Perca fluviatilis)* whose large numbers can be effectively reduced with the aid of a drag-net.

A boat makes angling easier on all large waters.

latively difficult fish to catch, mainly due to its 'moodiness' in the way it does or does not bait. Most anglers fish for the Pike-perch with a lead weight using a small live or dead fish for bait at the bottom, or a live fish in place of a float. Using this method, they wait for the Pike-perch to condescend and begin to forage for something to eat, and hope that the food they are offering him is to his taste. The deciding factors in this game are whether the angler has correctly guessed the

The Perch *(Perca fluviatilis)* is one of the most sought after objects of angling in valley reservoirs. Perch fishing in the autumn season is part of the traditional angling festivities that very few anglers miss.

Pike-perch's place of residence and whether it is hungry. Obviously the best precondition for success in fishing for the Pike-perch is knowledge of the water, including the underwater areas, and also sufficient time. So there is less chance of success for who have only come for a spot of weekend fishing or are on a short holiday hoping to catch a beautiful Pike-perch specimen.

Anglers try to find and become acquainted with the habitat of the Pike-perch and lure him to the bait at that site. The Pike-perch usu-

The Roach *(Rutilus rutilus)* is one of the most abundant of fish found in valley reservoirs. Hence Roach fishing is a highly enjoyable pastime offered by valley reservoirs, which can lead to surprise catches of 0.5–1.0 kg fish.

An autumn day on the reservoir. ▶

ally dwell in waters that are 6–12 m deep (in the autumn and winter months up to a depth of 15–20 m) near the original basin of the flooded river. These fish are often found in places with flooded stumps, scree or where a water current of a clean tributary enters the valley reservoir. From here they swim to places where there is sufficient food – particularly small fish. So this is the fishing ground for Pike-perch. These places are very often some sort of scree or stony

The sunset ends one angling day in a valley reservoir whose watery surface reflects the wake of the boat...

◄

slopes descending into the water where the Pike-perch move to in search of food. The Pike-perch fishing grounds are usually known among anglers but at these sites there is no other choice except to wait until the Pike-perch begin to hunt for food. Those anglers who are lucky and catch such a time later recall these moments as something totally unreal. To catch Pike-perch giants weighing 4–8 kg can disconcert even an experienced angler. A more effective way of catching a Pike-perch is by systematically searching out the place where the fish spends time hibernating and luring him with an appropriately selected bait. It is highly probable that any Pike-perch will not resist even a dragged bait if it comes into its angle of vision and disturbs its sleep. This is the angler's chance – he must carefully hook the fish and, after a short struggle, the elegant body of the Pike-perch will appear at the surface as the fish is forced to leave its habitat in the depths of the water. The greater the depth from which a Pike-perch is pulled out and the quicker the action, the less chance it has to defend itself, because it has no time to adjust to the different water pressures at a depth of 15–20 m and at the water surface. A Pike-perch pulled out from such a depth has a stiff inflated body with a swollen belly and the gullet is often right up in the mouth.

A very effective way of fishing for Pike-perch is by drag line, although this method is used by anglers less often than fishing with a live fish or lead weight. A 7–9 cm dead fish can be used as dragged bait, or even smaller spinners. One lets the dead fish fall right to the bottom and then drags it up from the bottom. During the course of this action one should shake the point from time to time, thereby giving the impression that the fish is injured and therefore good and accessible game for the Pike-perch. The line should be held steady but lightly when dragging it. As soon as some resistance is felt, one should stop pulling, and, after waiting a moment, gently pull the line again, and, as soon as slight resistance or jerking is felt, let the line go, release the lock of the reel, wait until the line begins to move and pull tight. We may even allow the fish to move on a bit or, as soon as we ascertain the direction of the pull and the line goes tight, we can hook the fish. In colder weather catching a Pike-perch by this method of dragging the line merely signals some sort of greater resistance as though the line were gaining in weight. This form of line dragging is very effective and, after mastering the technique, the increased efforts bring rewards in the greater size of the catch. A similar method – so-called vertical line-dragging, carried out from a boat or under the ice when the bait is lowered vertically and slowly pulled up and lowered again, also proves successful if one knows the habitat of the Pike-perch. The use of a boat when fishing for Pike-perch on a valley reservoir extends the possibilities and considerably increases the chances of success. Above all, it allows access to those places where the Pike-perch dwells when resting. When fishing for Pike-perch we must also be prepared for a catch of other deep-water predators such as the Pike, prime specimens of Perch or even the bearded underwater king, the European Catfish.

The valley reservoir is a unique underwater kingdom, where fish can live to a great age and grow to massive proportions, providing the potential to fulfil every angler's dream catch.

Lakes are naturally formed water areas of different origins distributed throughout the world. Some countries are sparse in lakes (e.g. the Czech Republic, Hungary), whereas others have abundant lakeland. For example, Finland is called the land of a thousand lakes and Scandinavia in general, as well as regions of northern Poland and the Alps, are well-known lake areas. In the warm lowlands on the Austro-Hungarian border lies the well-known lake, Neusiedler See, which covers an area of 320 km^2 which, in view of its small depth, is highly productive and famed for its wealth of fish. The largest lake in Europe is the vast Lake Ladoga situated in the northern part of Russia – its water area of 18,135 m^2 with an average depth of 50 m. The nearby Lake Onega also covers a large area (9,800 km^2). Most lakes are smaller. Due to the fact that lakes are created by nature, they blend with the landscape usually forming a very attractive prospect. Lake fishing has its own peculiarities. The fact remains that fishing on lakes, both for professional and amateur anglers, is a much more difficult and demanding matter than fishing on smaller reservoirs or brooks and rivers. The fish colony of lakes is varied according to the conditions in which the lake is found. Lakes with a population of Salmon fish are either situated at a considerable height above sea level or lie in northern parts of Europe. In Charr type lakes the Charr *(Salvelinus arcticus)* is obviously the main inhabitant. It lives together with the Lake Trout *(Salmo trutta morpha lacustris)*, several species of Whitefish and the Minnow. In many European lakes where the Lake Trout is found, other species can be found such as the Perch, Roach, Silver Bream and even the Pike or Pike-perch. In Whitefish type lakes various species or forms of Whitefish (e.g. *Coregonus lavaretus, C. nasus, C. oxyrhynchus, C. albula*) occur, as well as the Charr and Trout, but there are also greater numbers of the Perch, Pike and Roach, and the Eel is also common. Cyprinid type lakes are obviously dominated by cyprinid fishes such as the Common Bream and Roach together with the Perch and Pike, and the Pike-perch is also found in most of them. Only in shallow and eutrophic fish type lakes is there a greater abundance of the Carp or the Tench.

Lake angling has a beauty of its own and because it is often a part of a longer recreational stay, it is becoming a regular part of the annual holiday for many anglers. A boat is essential for lake fishing, en-

An advancing lake: a steep bank which the pounding waves are gnawing and eating away bit by bit.

A north German lake surrounded by sandy banks covered in low pine trees.

abling angling in those places where there is the greatest chance of a successful catch. Fishing in lakes is more difficult than on normal inland freshwaters and can even be dangerous if one is overcome by bad weather far from the shore. Every precaution should be taken when fishing on bigger lakes and this applies not only to safety considerations, but also to the approach adopted to fishing itself. The fish density in lakes is irregular. Large numbers of fish are usually found in places which suit them partly because of the character of the water, but mainly because there is sufficient food available. It is up to the angler to try to seek out such places and try his luck. Any information acquired from local experts about fishing possibilities is invaluable. Therefore one tries to save time by fishing in places where the presence of fish is guaranteed. For lake fishing heavier and longer fishing-rods and reels are used. This enables the angler to cast the line further, which is particularly important when fishing from the shore. The best places to seek out the fish are areas of aquatic vegetation, flooded obstacles, rugged rocks or warm shallow waters.

The Charr *(Salvelinus arcticus)* is found in the Alpine lakes and in the lakes of northern Europe, particularly in the British Isles, Scandinavia, Finland and Iceland. Outside Europe it is widespread in Alaska, North America and Japan. The Charr is one of the most beautiful fish of the Salmonidae family, with its elegant oblong body, dark olive coloured back, light greenish to silver sides with red spots and orange belly which turns dark blood red in colour during the spawning season. It finds the best living conditions in deep lakes with clean water. Although found in the Alps in mountain lakes at over 2,000 m (Lake Dossner at 2,280 m above sea level), in northern Europe it lives in lakes almost at sea level. It is also found in the coastal waters of the Norwegian fjords. It requires lakes that are at least 10 m deep and dwells mostly in the watery depths. Unlike its relative, the Brook Trout *(Salvelinus fontinalis)*, it hates acid waters.

In the Alpine lakes it exists in a number of ecological forms which differ in their reproduction season (December to January or July), in the form of nutrition which they consume (plankton or small fishes) and in their place of growth. Some ecological forms (often depending on the abundance and food conditions) measure up to 30 cm and weigh 0.5 kg, others measure 50–60 cm and weigh up to 3 kg, whereas sea migrating forms grow up to 80 cm in length and weigh several kilos.

Charr fishing is similar to the method used when fishing for other salmonids, either by dragging a line on a spinner or by fly-fishing using an artificial fly. In deep waters unexpected success can sometimes be achieved with deep vertical line dragging when the bait, usually a spinner, is lowered and raised vertically. A boat is essential for this method of fishing as it enables the angler to position himself above the habitat of the Charr in the depths of a lake. The Charr is of the greatest importance for fishing in the arctic northern lakes.

Another characteristic species found in many lakes is the Perch *(Perca fluviatilis)*, widespread in waters throughout Europe, with the exception of Scotland, Norway and the south European peninsulas. This fish can be encountered in virtually all types of waters with the exception of colder waters of a salmonid character.

The Perch represents the well-armed knight of the underwater fish world, covered in hard shell of coarse scales and equipped with

In some lakes the Freshwater Houting *(Coregonus lavaretus)* grows to trophy proportions (about 3 kg).

The Black Lake in the Bohemian Forest (the Czech Republic) dates back to the Ice Age and the water has a low pH value; only the Brook Trout *(Salvelinus fontinalis)* lives there.

A scree disappearing into the depths of a mountain lake serves as a fish habitat.

An exquisite male Brook Trout *(Salvelinus fontinalis)* catch proves that this species ranks among the most beautiful of freshwater fish.

prickly fins, including sharp thorns on the gill-covers (opercula). The high body with an arched back, wedge-shaped head with large eyes and the relatively large terminal finely toothed mouth enables it to devour really large pieces of food. It is yellowish-green to grey and brownish in colour with a metallic copper lustre on the sides. The ventral, pectoral and anal fins are a bright red colour. The dorsal fin is divided into two parts – the first is reinforced with prickles.

The Perch lives in shoals and only the largest fish become reclusive. It is a highly adaptable fish living in most types of fresh waters. It is unequalled in its voracity and devours every living thing that gets in its way. The smaller Perch fish live mainly on zooplankton, while the larger specimens, measuring 150–200 mm, become predators. A shoal of Perch can hunt for small fish like a pack of wolves – the shoal forms a sort of circle round these fishes, which, out of sheer terror, even jump out of the water onto the dry shore to try to escape. The Perch is a medium aged fish with the oldest specimens living for 15–20 years. They grow quite slowly, in five years reaching 150–250 mm in length and the biggest fish can reach a length of up

123

A lowland lake with reeds growing in shallow places – its waters contain the Carp, Common Bream, Roach, Perch, Pike-perch and other species.

to 600 mm and weigh 4–6 kg. The Perch reaches sexual maturity at the age of 1–3 years. The female is quite fertile – for 1 kg of her body weight she can spawn 150–200 eggs. The Perch spawns mainly in April and May when the spawned eggs are laid by the female in 1–2 m long strips on submerged aquatic plants, shrubs, branches or stones. In certain cases the Perch tends to over-reproduce, which reduces its intensity of growth, thus depreciating the value of the Perch population from the fishing point of view.

A prime specimen of the Lake Trout *(Salmo trutta morpha lacustris)* being netted by a lucky angler.

124

The Pike-perch *(Stizostedion lucioperca)* takes up the bait even when being dragged by various spinners.

In some lakes the Perch *(Perca fluviatilis)* grows to a substantial size.

A lucky angler returns to the bank after catching a large trout.

The Perch ranks among the favourite trophies of anglers. It has excellent, tasty meat, which is sought after by hotels in the Swiss and French lake resorts. One can fish for Perch in various ways. What is

A highly effective and frequently used fishing device in lakes are keep nets.

A catch with the use of mesh nets during ich-thyologic research enables us to acquire more detailed knowledge about the true state of fish habitats in a lake.

very effective is the dragging of smaller spinners with various red appendages. If the Perch begin to bite, one can catch 6–8 beautiful fishes in 10–15 minutes, because Perch live mainly in shoals. The Perch can also be enticed by a worm either by float-fishing or lead-weight.

The calm surface of the lake does not betray any of the secrets which it contains.

For drag fishing dead fish can also be used. A classic form of bait (if this is permissible) are small live fish - a small Perch, Moderlieschen or Roach - which it finds hard to resist. A small live fish, particularly a silvery Moderlieschen, seals the fate of these greedy predators. Anglers usually look for Perch in deeper water near flooded trees and rocks. Perch are only found in shallow waters in the summer months, when they go hunting like wolves for small fish spawn. A Perch catch weighing over 2 kg is the fulfilment of an angler's dreams.

When fishing for Perch in deep water from a boat or overhanging bank, it is recommended to try vertical dragging of a spinner or fake fish which often proves very successful. One can fish for Perch in a similar way in winter by lowering the spinner into the watery depths through a hole in the ice. A special short rod is required for this. This is a favourite method of fishing in northern Europe. When fishing for Perch one should be prepared for baiting other predators such as the Pike-perch or Pike.

In some shallow and warm lakes one also encounters the Carp *(Cyprinus carpio)*. This is usually Carp of various forms bred in fishponds. The original Wild Carp is only rarely found in big rivers such as in the middle or lower course of the River Danube. Carp fishing on lakes is also attractive because the chance of catching older specimens of Carp weighing 15-20 kg causes many followers of St. Peter's Guild a sleepless night. The greatest chances of catching Carp are offered by those places where the Carp go to fatten up. These are usually shallow areas only up to 2 m deep with a boggy bottom and water vegetation. If one goes fishing at such a site frequently, it is good to entice Carp to the site by regular feeding. One fishes for carp either with a float or lead weight using dough, corn, peas, bread or baked potatoes. For Carp fishing one uses a longer rod measuring over 3 m with a bigger reel and sufficient line that is 0.25-0.30 mm thick. If one is not fishing from a boat one casts to a distance of 50-100 m, although the Carp will swim right up to the bank in its search for food. A struggle with the Carp is always a battle because it is a tough opponent and overpowering a larger Carp weighing over 10 kg is a knee-trembling experience. The Carp has become a symbol of fishing for many anglers although it is only found in a lot of waters thanks to released fry bred in fishponds.

In many cases, beautiful and clean lakes are becoming a thing of the past. Human activity is causing the gradual diminishment of water purity. This has also caused a change in the fish fauna. In polluted waters Salmonids and Whitefish are replaced by more tolerant species of fish which are of lower quality, particularly from the *Cyprinidae* family. A very complicated process of lake pollution - eutrophication - as a consequence of human activity, has been taking place in recent years at such a rate that it spells ecological catastrophe. A particular and almost insoluble problem is water acidification as a consequence of the presence of sulphuric oxides in the form of acid rain. The rainfall is transforming the water environment into a weak solution of sulphuric acid. Many northern lakes, as a consequence of the fall in the pH value of the water to 3-4, have lost their fish fauna and these lakes have, instead, become dead waters. Water pollution, lake devastation and the disappearance of their fish colonies - all this has roused human society, regardless of nationality, to join forces to put an end gradually to the pollution of lake waters.

FISHPONDS

Trees lean over the watery surface of a fishpond as though guarding the wealth of fish that the pond contains. Carp, Tench, Pike and Pike-perch plough through the water undisturbed foraging for food.

The origin and development of fish breeding is closely connected with and conditioned by the construction of artificial water reservoirs – fishponds. Fish breeding originated in ancient times in China. The first people in Europe to engage in fish breeding were the ancient Romans at the beginning of our millennium. Columella (in the first century A.D.) writes that the Romans not only kept and fed fishes in fishponds but also undertook breeding. After the fall of the Roman Empire, it was, above all, the monasteries and then later the aristocracy, yeomen and the townships which contributed towards the continuing construction of fishponds. Many fishponds, which even now still form a part of big fishpond systems, were constructed in central Europe in the 13th –15th century. Many of them have been preserved and are proof of the art of building craftsmanship and the courage of medieval builders. Some of them have the character of valley reservoirs.

Fishponds were originally built on swamp ground that was not very fertile. The fish yield of these fishponds brought considerable income for their owners. The golden age in the development and construction of fishponds in central Europe was interrupted by the Thirty Years' War. During the 19th and 20th century many fishponds were transformed into arable land. Those fishponds that remained became the basis of fish breeding for that part of the fishing industry which we call fish farming. Most fishponds are located in the countries of central Europe: the Czech Republic, Poland, Germany, Hungary, Austria, and also France and former Yugoslavia. Other countries have smaller-sized fishponds used for intensive Salmon breeding.

Fishpond construction is connected with the development of fish breeding, especially of the Carp, Tench and Pike-perch. At the end of the 19th century and particularly in recent decades, Europe witnessed the breeding of acclimatized fishes. These include not only salmonids such as the Rainbow Trout, but herbivorous fishes too. The development of fish breeding in fishponds was always influenced by the period and the prevailing socio-economic circumstances. In contemporary times, fish farming – fish breeding in fishponds – has experienced fundamental changes. New knowledge, the utilization of a broad spectrum of intensifying procedures and methods (fertilization, feeding, breeding, mixing of various species of fry) have led to

131

a situation whereby the annual production of fishponds gradually increased from the original 100–200 kg per hectare to 800–1,500 kg per hectare and even these yields are not considered the uppermost limit. Breeding in fishponds at the present time has taken on, in many respects, the character of intensive agricultural production. However, it is strongly affected by natural conditions and has therefore retained its biological character.

The predominant fish bred in European fishponds since the beginning of their construction and use, has been the Carp because its qualities – rapid growth, robustness, good meat quality – are best suited to fishing requirements. Even in contemporary times, now that the fishpond population has been extended to include other species so it does not solely consist of the Carp, this species remains the main object of fishpond production. This species merits a closer look, because it is not just the object of human consumption, as it tends to be a favourite fish among sporting anglers and is bred in fishponds for their enjoyment.

In Europe the Carp originated in the big rivers flowing into the Caspian, Black and Mediterranean Seas. Of course the Carp is even considered an original inhabitant of the Rhine. As far back as the first century A.D. the Romans began breeding Carp in artificial reservoirs called fishponds. At the present time the Carp is widespread in waters throughout the world. The original Wild Carp form is now only found in some big European rivers (e.g. the Danube, Tisa, Rhine). The Wild Carp is a highly endangered species. In most waters now, so-called cultured forms of Carp are found that have been artificially refined after many years of breeding. The Carp has literally passed through a domesticating process. Refined, cultured forms or actual Carp breeds are usually distinguished by their high body and excellent growth qualities. They have very well developed adaptability and survival capabilities. Likewise the flesh also has an excellent taste. The cultured forms of Carp are refined for intensive breeding with a great amount of fry and intensive feeding.

The Carp has a robust body that is either fully or partially covered in large scales – the scaly Carp – or there is the bald or scaleless – mirror and leather Carp. The short powerful head has a ventral mouth consisting of movable and protruding lips forming a kind of snout for collecting food. Four barbels are found at the corners of the upper lip. The Carp has powerful fins classically arranged on the body. The dorsal fin is very wide. The colouring of the Carp is variable as far as the shading is concerned. The back tends to be dark green, grey or greyish blue, the sides usually have a yellowish green to golden hue, the belly tends to be whitish or yellowish white. The fins are a greyish blue except for the anal and caudal ones which are reddish in colour. From the point of view of the colouring, there are various refined local forms such as the 'blue' or the 'grey' Carp. The special decorative form of Carp – the koy – actually represents one of the most refined cultured forms of this species.

Although the Carp is a highly adaptable fish, it does not like flowing water. Its original biotope is the downstream of big rivers with a rich system of inundated waters, pools, lakes and branches. The Carp finds the best environment in shallow, eutrophic reservoirs with a slightly swampy bed that is partly covered with aquatic plants. Fishponds provide it with the best artificially created conditions. The Carp

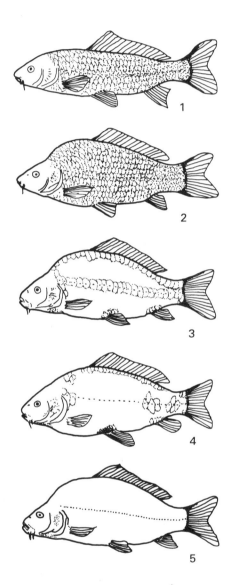

The Carp (*Cyprinus carpio*): 1 – the original wild form living in the lowland parts of big rivers is completely covered in scales with a cylindrical body. Refined forms have a high body: 2 – the scaly Carp, 3 – the scaleless Carp with one row of scales, 4 – the bald (scaleless) Carp, 5 – the smooth (scaleless) Carp.

Secluded spots in a fishpond surrounded by
bushes and trees as well as stretches of aquatic plants on the banks all create an idyllic environment. Fishponds – originally artificial
reservoirs – were gradually incorporated into
nature so successfully that they are now considered an integral part of it.

133

lives in shoals and its activity is usually restricted by a temperature fall to below 5–7°C. In winter, when the water surface freezes over, it retires to deeper sites where it waits for winter to pass in a sort of state of hibernation.

At first the Carp fry live off zooplankton *(Cladocera* and *Cyclopoidea),* but very soon begin to search for food at the bottom in the same way as the older fish. The Carp is a typical benthophage because it searches out various benthonic organisms for food such as the larvae of *Chironomidae* and other aquatic invertebrates. A significant part of the Carp's food are certain sections of plants, particularly various seeds. These, mainly corn and other seeds, form its main food which is used for Carp breeding.

Gathering in the fish from a fishpond is a hard day's work. ▶

134

Autumn is here – the fish farming harvest. The water is let out of the fishponds and fish farmers begin to haul in the fish. A large net – the drag-net – is pulled in at each side so that a plentiful amount of fish remain in the net. ◄

In rare instances the Carp may live for 20 to 30 years. It has very good growth capabilities depending on the length of the growing season and availability of food. The Carp is a thermophilic species whose metabolic optimum water temperature ranges between 18-25°C. In the conditions of central Europe, the cultured breed of Carp usually grows to 10-15 cm and weighs up to 0.15 kg. Three-year olds, depending on the conditions and amount of food, can attain a length of 25-40 cm and weigh 1.5-3.0 kg. Catches of re-

The haul of the drag-net is over, the fish are enclosed in the net and await collection.

cord specimens, from shallow, eutrophic valley reservoirs in Europe, weigh 20–30 kg.

The Carp reaches sexual maturity at the age of 2–4 years. The female is very fertile. Spawning takes place in groups when the water temperature reaches 17–20°C which usually occurs at the end of May

Thousands of fish imprisoned in the drag-net, agitated and trying to escape.

A mechanical landing-net hauls out catch after catch from the masses of fish enclosed in the drag-net which is surrounded by a circle of small fishing boats. The fishpond is yielding its annual harvest. One such haul with a drag-net may land a hundredweight of fish and it may take a whole day before such a haul is completed.

or in June. The Carp is a typical phytophilic fish that requires aquatic plants for spawning, to which it attaches its eggs. The development of the fertilized eggs lasts 2.5–5 days depending on the water temperature. Nowadays artificial spawning is carried out in Carp breeding with the aid of hypophysation. The spawned and fertilized eggs are hatched in conical hatching tanks containing several dozens of litres. Artificial reproduction has removed the freaks of nature from the results of Carp reproduction.

Most Carp 'production' is attained within the scope of its breeding in fishponds. In European market conditions, the Carp becomes a consumer product at the age of three, some individuals a year older or younger weighing 1.5–4.0 kg each. In a number of countries the Carp represents the traditional Christmas menu. Apart from Carp bred for consumption, part of the production of fry in fishponds is released into natural waters. Some of the fish which are released into so-called fishing districts, attain game size and become the object of angling.

At fishponds where there is no mechanization, fish are hauled in by manual landing-nets and submitted for selection and sorting.

Fishing tackle used for hauling in the contents of a fishpond. Fish picked from the drag-net are put in a tub where they are weighed, and then proceed to transport crates filled with water and finally it's farewell to the fishpond.

The Carp as an object of angling is usually valued as a relatively high commodity. Basically there are two ways of fishing for Carp – with lead weight or by float-fishing. Baits used are usually forms of vegetation or specially prepared dough. The Carp usually bites the bait sharply and after being caught on the rod and line it fights persistently and tenaciously. Catching bigger fishes with a fine fishing tackle is an appreciable sporting feat.

Although the Carp is the main fish bred in fishponds, it is not the only species forming their populations. Even in earlier times, apart from the Carp, the regular members of the fishpond colony also included other species of fish. They used to get into the fishponds by

139

chance from the surrounding waters. But fish farmers soon recognized that some of these species were a welcome addition to the fishpond population of fish and began to cultivate them in the fishponds deliberately.

Above all, predators (the Pike and Pike-perch) found their use in the fishpond population as they suppressed and restricted the occurrence of other undesirable species which the fish farmer describes as weed species – i.e. the Roach, the Rudd, the Moderlieschen, the Common Bream, the Perch, the Ruffe etc. – but which are being sought after more and more as fry for angling waters. The Tench holds a significant place in the fishpond population. Further species of fish gradually began to be used in fish breeding, several of which were imported into Europe from other geographical regions.

Above all, the Rainbow Trout, which was imported in the 19th century from North America, was quickly introduced. The Rainbow Trout became the most important species of fish farming production besides the Carp. It is reared in special, smaller trout fishponds or in aqua-culture facilities or it may be placed in fishponds with colder water as an additional fish apart from the Carp. In the last century the Freshwater Houting *(Coregonus lavaretus)* was successfully utilized in deep and colder fishponds, and in recent years another species of

The scaly Carp *(Cyprinus carpio)* – mother fish.

The embankments of large fishponds are reinforced with enormous trees – mainly oaks which have outlived several human generations.

In Japan these multicoloured forms of Carp have been bred for decorative purposes.

The Tench *(Tinca tinca)* is a significant species bred in fishponds together with the Carp. Above is the female, heavy with eggs, below the male with his powerful ventral fins.

Whitefish, the Siberian Peled *(Coregonus peled)* has been successfully introduced to fishponds. Whitefish have very high quality meat and have become a valuable addition to the fish population of fishponds.

Fish fauna cultivated in European fishponds has, in recent years, been enriched with further species imported from different geographical regions; at the top the Siberian Peled or Northern Peled *(Coregonus peled)* and below the Silver Carp *(Hypophthalmichthys molitrix).*

Fishponds have become an integral part of nature and are proof of the building craftsmanship and the courage of medieval builders.

There were unsuccessful attempts at rearing the Horned Pout *(Ictalurus nebulosus)* in fishponds, which was also imported from North America. After 1960 three species were imported from eastern Asia which can be described as herbivores. One of these species of fish is the Grass Carp *(Ctenopharyngodon idella)* which can feed on taller aquatic plants and if its population is sufficiently dense, it can remove any undesirable growths in fishponds. This species appears to be very useful because, apart from the fact that it upgrades the vegetation, it also fulfils the biomelioration function by preventing the undesirable overgrowth of fishponds with aquatic plants. This previously had to be suppressed either in a mechanical way (cutting out) or by chemical sprays, but these proved totally unsuitable from an ecological point of view. There are other species, the Silver Carp *(Hypophthalmichthys molitrix)* and the Bighead Carp *(Aristichthys nobilis)*. The first of these feeds mainly on phytoplankton *(algae* and *Cyanophyta)*, the second on zooplankton. Both species grow very well both in still waters and in big rivers.

143

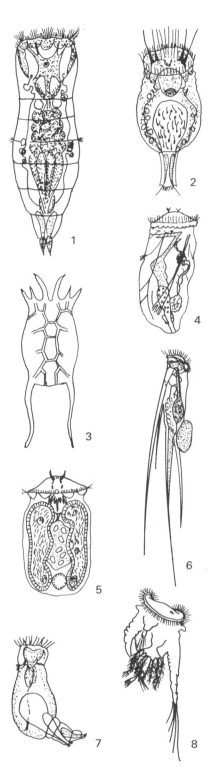

Another related species imported from eastern Asia – the Bighead Carp *(Aristichthys nobilis)* – is doing well in European waters.

For example, individual specimens weighing up to 25 kg have been caught downstream in the Danube river tributaries in Slovakia. All three species of these herbivore fishes do not naturally reproduce in Europe and their occurrence is maintained only through artificial reproduction. The intensive growth of fish farming production has virtually removed the Largemouth Bass *(Micropterus salmoides)* which was imported from North America in the last century and is still only found in a few European countries. Apart from the predatory fish already mentioned, fish farmers also managed to introduce the European Catfish *(Silurus glanis)* into fishponds on a wider scale after its successful artificial reproduction.

Fish breeding in fishponds was always a source and inspiration for the import of fishes from a different geographical region. Although efforts to acclimatize some new species proved successful, several species were introduced (see above) which can be regarded as a positive contribution to fish farming and European ichthyofauna. The implementation of further species of fish in polycultures, together with the Carp, enables the far more effective production capabilities of fishponds, stock of natu-

Microzooplankton is made up of very small creatures and represents the most important and irreplaceable food for the youngest fishes after they hatch. The most important are the *Rotatoria*: 1 – *Epiphanes senta*, 2 – *Ceratella cochlearis*, 3 – *Ceratella quadrata*, 4 – *Asplancha priodenta*, 5 – *Ascomorpha acaudis*, 6 – *Tetramastix opoliensis*, 7 – *Brachionus rubens*, 8 – *Hexarthra mira*.

Another part of Far East Asian ichthyofauna which was imported more than 20 years ago to European waters – the Grass Carp *(Cteno-pharyngodon idella)*. It was introduced to fishponds mainly to restrain the abundant aquatic plant life.

ral food and better utilization of used fodder. It is polycultures which bring fish farmers an increase in fish production by 50–200 % as opposed to the net carp population.

Fishponds have become an integral part of nature. They accumu-

The fishpond banks are bordered by a certain type of aquatic plant: the *Sparganium ramosum* – in the picture, the Reed *(Phragmites communis)*, the *Glyceria aquatica*, the Reedmace *(Typha)*, the Sweet Sedge *(Acorus calamus)*, the Bent-grass *(Carex)* etc.

The Largemouth Bass *(Micropterus salmoides)* was imported into Europe in the last century from North America and is still bred in some south Bohemian fishponds.

late large volumes of water and significantly contribute to the hydrological system of the entire region. The importance of fishponds should not only be seen in the sphere of fish breeding as fishponds

The Freshwater Houting and the Siberian Peled *(Coregonus levaretus* and *Coregonus peled* – in the picture) have been bred successfully in colder fishponds where they complement the Carp population.

also provide a suitable environment for many species of water birds. Dozens of mammals as well as songbirds also live in the reeds. In many regions where fishponds have existed for centuries, fishponds have literally blended with the landscape. The multipurpose nature of most fishponds has considerably increased their value, therefore their area should continue to expand.

The low water level of the fishpond, falling leaves and the overall view indicate the forthcoming autumn days.

A meal around the fire provides a pleasant end
to the angling day.

FISH IN WINTER

Winter is the season of snow and ice, sudden turns and changes, the season when nature reduces its intensity of life to a minimum, when not only plants but also many creatures go into hibernation. The water surface of reservoirs, lakes and fishponds is mostly encased in a cover of ice as are brooks and rivers. The water temperature in winter ranges between 0°C–4°C and because the body temperature of fishes is basically determined by the temperature of the surrounding environment, the bodily and life functions of most species of fish are considerably reduced. The intensity of the matter metabolism falls in many species of fish to a minimum, so if fish hibernate, they may survive the entire winter season from December to March without consuming any food.

Other species which live, above all, in flowing waters, must, however, remain active and generate energy so that they are not victims of the water current. There are even fish which are most active in the winter season and their activity culminates in reproduction – spawning.

Fish which live in flowing water must receive food even in winter to compensate for the energy they discharge when in motion and sustaining their position in the current. Typical examples of such fish are the Nase *(Chrondrostoma nasus)*, the Dace *(Leuciscus leuciscus)*, the Chub *(Leuciscus cephalus)* and the *Alburnoides bipunctatus.* But there are fish which go into hibernation in still waters, that remain in motion in flowing waters. Hence we might catch a Common Bream *(Abramis brama)*, a Roach *(Rutilus rutilus)* and even a Carp *(Cyprinus carpio)* at the beginning of the winter season. In winter those fishes are also active which thrive best in cooler waters. The optimum water temperature ranges from 8°C to 15°C. This applies, above all, to salmonids. Brown Trout *(Salmo trutta fario)* spawning, in some years lasts until December or even January. The Rainbow Trout *(Salmo gairdneri)* keenly forages for food to prepare for early spring spawning, just like the Huchen *(Hucho hucho)* or the Grayling *(Thymallus thymallus)*. Whitefish *(Coregonidae)* often spend their nuptials at the beginning of winter under the ice covered water surface and lay fertilized eggs on the sandy lake bed. In two to three months small fry hatch from these eggs often still beneath the ice cover. The activity of Salmonids and Whitefish shows that these fish do not take hibernation too seriously. On the contrary, a typical winter sleeper in flowing waters is the Barbel *(Barbus barbus)*. In the late autumn it seeks out deeper areas with a stony or rocky bottom and layers of foliage. It is here that it literally buries itself in the leaves and passes the winter in hibernation to be woken up by the early spring flood waters. Downstream, where the actual river basin is connected to several side pools and blind river branches, a number of species such as the Carp, Common Bream, Crucian Carp, Tench as well as the European Catfish or Pike-perch seek out quiet spots in valley reservoirs, lakes and fishponds, that is to say, in stagnant water where they spend the winter in relative calm right through until spring.

Fish which do not consume food during hibernation, must, of course, prepare for this fast of several months. Therefore they eat intensively in the summer and autumn, thus increasing their energy and body weight, created mainly of fat. At the beginning of spring, after the end of winter these fishes are really emaciated, but they very soon wipe out the effects of hibernation with a sufficient supply of food.

Anglers do not give up visits to water sites even in winter because winter fishing with a rod and line has a magic all of its own despite the somewhat harsher conditions – the cold and frost. Winter fishing has its own peculiarities which have to be taken into consideration in order to achieve success. In flowing and unfrozen still waters one concentrates, above all, on catching fish which are known to be active even in winter water – e.g. the Roach, the Chub, the Nase as well as the Common Bream, the Perch and the Burbot. However, there is always the possibility that a totally unexpected fish such as the Carp, can take the bait. Fish are less active in colder waters and therefore take the bait sluggishly, cautiously and hesitantly. The most successful fishing in winter is float-fishing when one uses fine tackle – a longer rod (3–4 m), smaller reel, a 0.5–0.20 m line, a fine float and smaller hooks. Breadcrumbs, small worms, white maggots, etc. are used as bait. In the winter season one should search for fish in relatively peaceful places such as on the border between a current and quiet waters where flowing water merges into pools or deeper quiet spots. When fishing one should observe the float carefully and a slight quiver signals that the fish has taken the bait. One can use poultry intestines or sausages to catch the Chub by impaling these on a hook and fishing around in each pool in turn, carefully using the bait to entice the fish. Catching a large Chub at this time of the year is a truly marvellous reward for these efforts.

A specific form of winter fishing is that carried out on ice when the bait is lowered down into cut out or drilled holes in the ice. In some countries this method of winter fishing is prohibited for safety reasons. Winter fishing down holes in the ice is widespread, above all, in northen parts of Europe. A relatively short and hard rod with a simple reel is used. The bait either consists of various spinners or worms, or hooks with small glittering pieces of metal (fake fish) or `a dead fish. Such bait is lowered through a hole in the ice, right down to the bottom and gradually raised and lowered again. This is basically a form of drag-fishing. This is a successful form of fishing for catching the Burbot as well as the gluttonous Perch, sometimes even the Pike or Rainbow Trout. What does the gloomy water lake kingdom look like in the stagnant waters beneath the ice? In winter fish retire to deep water areas where they hibernate. Certain species, particularly cyprinid *(Cyprinidae)* fishes, hibernate in winter to wait for the passing of this, for them, unfavourable season. However, even in winter, in stagnant waters there are fish which are constantly active although they are more hesitant than in warmer seasons of the year. Above all, these are cold-loving fishes such as the Rainbow Trout, the Freshwater Houting *(Coregonus lavaretus)*, the Siberian Peled *(C. peled)*, the Vendace *(C. albula)* as well as the Lake Trout *(Salmo trutta m. lacustris)*. Also the Burbot and the Perch keenly forage for food in winter, hence we can successfully fish for them beneath the ice with a rod and line. Professional fishermen fish with nets beneath

A river in the winter season possesses tremendous beauty and charm even though it might stir up memories of fishing in the warmer seasons.

151

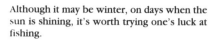
Although it may be winter, on days when the sun is shining, it's worth trying one's luck at fishing.

the ice in winter often with more success than in the summer, particularly when they know the fishes' winter gathering site.

Let us now take a look beneath the ice cover of one pool through the eyes of a diver. At a depth of 2 or more metres we can observe

The Rainbow Trout *(Salmo gairdneri)* does not rest in winter unlike many other fish species. So with a bit of luck an angler can take pleasure in a beautiful catch.

A small brook almost completely disappears beneath the winter covering of snow and only the water current glistening in places indicates that aquatic life in flowing waters does not stop even in winter.

A winter Common Bream catch *(Abramis brama)* proves that winter fishing can be successful.

various large Catfish whose heads appear to be buried in the muddy bottom. Their winter sleep is so deep that you can even touch their bodies or pull at their barbels and they do not even react to reflector lights. The Carp, in its deep hibernation, leans with its belly against the bottom, its body covered in fine detritus. The Pike-perch are found either alone or in groups sitting on their bellies on the lake bottom with their dorsal fins folded on their backs. Tench are also partly buried in the swampy detritus which appears to act as their mask. The Roach stands in shoals above the bottom and does not display any interest in the surroundings. The Pike, although reacting rather more slowly, does follow our movements and promptly retires to a safe distance. The Perch, remaining in shoals, are constantly active and lively in their movements. The Crucian Carp is perfectly masked in the roots of reed-mace and reeds and can only be spotted towards the end of this underwater excursion. In winter fish either hibernate

The watery depths of still waters encased in an ice shield which also bears layers of snow. A period of rest and winter hibernation in the gloom beneath the ice cover.　　▶

◄
A winter view at a submontane Huchen river in the region of the High Tatras (Slovakia).

on their own or in shoals. In places in fishponds, where Carp have hibernated in winter, in spring we can find large bowl-shaped hollows at the bottom – their winter beds.

The Burbot *(Lota lota)* is the only freshwater fish in European waters which is highly active in the winter season, because it reproduces in winter. It is the sole representative of Codfishes *(Gadidae)* living permanently in fresh inland waters north of the 45°C latitude. It lives a secluded life so its occurrence often escapes our attention. The wide flat head with the single barbel on the bottom jaw indicates that the Burbot is a predator which can devour large pieces of food. For most of the year it stays hidden under banks, between stones and

155

in holes only foraging for food at night. Its food foraging activity increases with the oncoming winter, culminating at the end of December and with the reproduction process in January. During spawning the male and female form many balls or clumps in shallow places with a sandy or scree bottom which catch the falling fertilized eggs. These are very small, about 1.0–1.5 mm in diameter. After about 60 days a sac embryo hatches from these fertilized eggs thus giving rise to a new generation of Burbot fishes. The Burbot is a highly fertile fish – the female releases more than 500,000 eggs per 1 kg of her body weight. After spawning, the parent fish return to their habitat in a pool or reservoir which they had left for the spawning grounds where they select the best conditions for the first days of the lives of their

An attempted catch with the use of a mesh under the ice of the valley reservoir lake indicates which fish are active even in winter. It is these species that, in their search for food, become entangled in the fine mesh fibres.

Winter angling through small holes in the ice cover tends to be successful above all in Perch fishing *(Perca fluviatilis)*. The Perch is caught by a special type of bait which is raised and lowered vertically.

Special fishing tackle for winter angling beneath the ice: a short fishing-rod with a simple reel, a special auger for drilling holes in the ice.

offspring. Great losses in eggs and, in the first days and weeks, of the Burbot fry mean that there is not an over-abundance of these fish.

The Burbot grows relatively quickly; in the first year it grows 80–150 mm, in the third year it measures 200–400 mm and in the fifth year 350–500 mm. The biggest specimens may grow to as much as 800 mm in length and weigh up to 4 kg. But these are truly prime specimens which would make every angler happy if caught. Burbot are caught by using a maggot or a live or dead fish. One should try to bring the bait as close to its habitat as possible, that is to say the shelters where the Burbot lies hidden. One fishes with a zinc weight. The Burbot does not become active till evening or at night, therefore there is a good chance of catching it at this time. Likewise if the water is cloudy the Burbot does not remain in its shelter and begins to forage for food, so there is also a chance of catching it during the

158

The resulting catch – some beautiful Burbot specimens *(Lota lota)* – demonstrates that the winter season is the best time to catch this fish.

◄
A lucky hunter in the final stage of a struggle with a prime Burbot catch on the ice cover of the reservoir.

day. With the oncoming winter, the voracity of the Burbot increases so the chances of catching it increase. The end of December and beginning of January, just before spawning, is the best time for the most successful Burbot catch. In reservoirs where the Burbot is found, one can fish for them successfully by using a live or dead fish as bait, which is lowered through a hole cut out in the ice. The Burbot has very delicate white dry meat, and large Burbot liver, resembling the liver of the Cod, is considered a delicacy.

The winter brings with it many problems and considerable danger for fishes. A considerable decrease in oxygen dissolved in water results beneath the frozen water surface particularly in waters with a rich content of organic matter or an abundance of aquatic plants. Apart from fishes and other remaining live organisms (e.g. zooplankton), plants or organic matter also contribute to the consumption of oxygen while the ice cover prevents more oxygen from entering the water. The ice, covered in a layer of snow, also prevents light from entering thus even the production of oxygen through as-

159

similation by green organisms (algae, plants) is also made impossible. For these reasons in the course of winter, the fish population may end up suffocating especially in stagnant waters. Hence in winter we

If the sun does appear, then the fish do bait a bit and winter angling on the ice cover of a lake is a great experience, especially in view of the picturesque winter scenery.

A prime specimen of a Burbot caught from beneath the ice.

An angler departs from an ice-bound lake after some successful fishing – he will return again in the spring.

cut holes in ice covered pools, smaller reservoirs, fishponds and lakes. We apply special instruments. These instruments, by moving and rippling the water surface, prevent it from freezing up. In case the content of dissolved oxygen in the water beneath the ice falls to a dangerous level (2.0–1.0 mg per litre), we try to actively replace the missing oxygen and oxygenate the water and remove dangerous products (e.g. methane, hydrogen sulphide). In such cases we apply special oxygenating instruments such as turboblowers, aerators or we drive air or oxygen from pressure tanks directly under the ice. Our struggle with the winter threat of the suffocation of fishes may be successful only in smaller water areas where it is in our power to eliminate the unfavourable conditions and replace the missing oxygen. The most effective method is a sufficient inflow of good oxygenated water. If winters are very harsh then even shallow waters may freeze over, thus resulting in the fish freezing.

Even flowing waters – brooks and rivulets – may freeze over, with a great frost, and then the fish have no chance of survival in the winter. But not even the end of winter means the end of problems for the fish. It is at this time that in rivers and brooks, with the increased water flows, ice-floes occur which may result in ice drifting, breaking up and killing many fishes. The end of winter means a fresh awakening for those fish which survive and which make sure that the water comes to life again with small fish fry.

MAN AND FISH

Fish stand at the very beginning and man at the climax of the evolution of vertebrates. The relationship of man with fish has, in the course of the passing centuries, evolved and extended in new aspects. In the distant past man's only relationship to fish was as a hunter. He caught fish mainly for food. The effect of man on fish and the water world at that time was so negligible that it was possible to catch fish and their numbers would naturally reproduce or be renewed. Over the course of time, with the development of human society, conditions changed so much that in man's relationship towards fish new and different elements have appeared. By introducing new methods and techniques, man has perfected fishing to such a degree that he is capable, under certain circumstances, of just removing fish from the waters. A new motivation has entered into fishing with a rod and line which is now just about equal to the original hunting motive: apart from the fact that man fishes for the purpose of consumption, angling has become an important form of active recreation and a way to regenerate the resources of the angler. The development of human society has caused man to begin to affect nature and the water environment in a negative way. In view of the fact that water is the sole and exclusive world for fish, the negative anthropogenic effects (above all water pollution, intervention in river hydrology, etc.), making the water environment worse, have far-reaching consequences for fish. Man began fish breeding soon after the original fishing activity. He gradually developed it in such a way that this part of fishing activity has become an important source of fish as a product for consumption and for populating open waters with fish. In this way man is trying to regenerate the affected fish colonies in open waters. Man's recent activities have made an important contribution towards the formation of suitable, sometimes new environments for fish.

Protection of Fish

The influence of man on the natural water ecosystems has become so damaging that he is now directly endangering the existence of several species of fish. Although the negative effect of man's activities is for the most part unintentional, in spite of or, possibly, because of this, its impact on fish fauna is often highly destructive and even catastrophic. There is no need to present examples of water courses, reservoirs or lakes, which, as a result of pollution, contain virtually no fish and have been transformed into sewers or decaying reservoirs: newspapers bring regular reports of fish being poisoned in our waters. By regulating river courses, altering their hydrological regime, constructing water structures (canals, dams, levels, etc.) man has changed the original ecological conditions so much that he has made it impossible for many species to survive and a fundamental change is occurring in the distribution of original fish species. How-

We all possess the latent instinct of the hunter inherited from our ancestors and this is reawakened during a spot of angling. Although today's conditions and the fishing tackle are totally different from the distant past, the desire to catch something remains as strong.

These days an undisturbed river with the original natural riverbed and relatively clean water is a rarity in most regions.

European Catfish *(Silurus glanis)* – the goal of every angler.

The clear blue surface of a mountain lake – a natural reserve of pure, unpolluted water.

ever, man's effect on fish does not, of course, only have negative aspects. Many interventions and activities by human society can be considered as positive with regard to the survival of fish in open waters. Man, or rather human society in general, is aware that, although at present he is unable to 'neutralize' the negative effects of his activities on fish fauna, he must make the maximum effort to preserve the existing species diversity of the original ichthyofauna of European waters, and, by gradually improving the production conditions in freshwater systems, he must renew the original, currently disturbed ichthyocenoses. An important aspect of efforts to preserve the original ichthyofauna is fish protection which should become an integral part of fishing activity in all types of waters.

A fish catch in the meshes of a professional net at the Lipno valley reservoir in the Bohemian Forest. In the background, a floating cage for feeding the Rainbow Trout.

The protection of fish has two goals. The first is to preserve the individual species which are in danger of extinction. The second is the protection of fish families and the species diversity, with particular consideration of the economic point of view.

At present, the European freshwater fish fauna consists of about 200 species, of which about 25 species were introduced to Europe from other geographical regions and have successfully acclimatized to European waters. About 30 % of species of fish living in European waters is, in varying degrees, directly endangered as far as their survival is concerned. About 10 species of fishes, such as the Huchen *(Hucho hucho)*, the Sturgeon *(Acipenseridae)*, the Salmon *(Salmo salar)*, the Mudminnow *(Umbra krameri)*, now fall into the category of highly endangered species in view of the state of their populations, area of occurrence and low ecological adaptability. For example, the present occurrence of the Huchen *(Hucho hucho)* is being preserved only by means of artificial reproduction and breeding. So under the present circumstances, as the quality of the water environment gradually deteriorates, the continued protection and care of the European ichthyofauna is of fundamental importance.

The meshes of the net are too small, so only the longer Bleak *(Alburnus alburnus)* that attempted to swim through the net were caught.

166

The protection of fish takes the form of a series of complex measures aiming to maintain and preserve the original species within their natural environment and territory. The most important element of these measures is the maintenance of the proper quality of the water and water environment as a whole. In view of the biological-ecological properties of fish, the most effective steps to be taken with regard to fish protection are as follows:

A catch of small cyprinid fishes (mainly the Bleak) used for feeding Rainbow Trout.

168

Man's interference in nature is not always favourable for fish. This view of a regulated stream bed shows the unfortunate consequences for the fish population.

A dam wall on a river has created an invincible obstacle for fish migrating upstream from the sea against the river current.

- Protection of the water biotopes (water courses, reservoirs, lake and canal systems, etc.) where an endangered species lives. Protection must be aimed particularly at preserving the proper quality of the water, the original water biotopes including the preservation of its water regime and character. Even the system of fishing management of the water systems in question must be subjected to the plan for protection of endangered species of fishes.
- The management and introduction of artificial breeding of those species of fish whose existence is endangered even though there might not be any immediate economic interest in breeding and managing these species. These measures, along with the regeneration of the ichthyofauna in devastated

Fishing with the aid of an electric current produced by a unit is very effective. It is used for ichthyologic research and for catching the female fish used for artificial spawning.

Electro-fishing helps us to obtain a clearer idea about the distribution of fish, particularly in smaller courses. Fish stunned by an electric current float to the surface, others try to escape from the field of the electric current.

A female Asp *(Aspius aspius)* caught in a river with the aid of electro-fishing for use in artificual spawning.

water biotopes, will enable the renewal of the occurrence of other species, as well as the economically important species – the Brown Trout *(Salmo trutta fario)*, the Nase *(Chondrostoma nasus)*, the Barbel *(Barbus barbus)*, the Orfe *(Leuciscus idus)* and the Burbot *(Lota lota)*], but which are not the object of fishing interests. This group includes species of the Minnow family *(Phoxinus)*, the Mudminnow *(Umbra)*, the *Alburnoides Dipunctatus*, the Gudgeon *(Gobio)* the Spined Loach *(Cobitis)*, the Ruffe *(Gymnocephalus)*, the Perch *(Romanichthys)*, the *Zingel zingel* and the Bullhead *(Cottus)*.

- Short-term selective protection of spawning grounds during the reproduction period in species with mass spawning (the Grayling – *Thymallus thymallus*, the Nase – *Chondrostoma nasus, Ch. toxostoma*, etc.).
- The regulation of water courses and human intervention in the water biotopes are damaging to fish and always result in a deterioration in their living conditions. Now, as a result of pressure from anglers, biologists and ecologists, so-called biotechnical projects for the regulation of water courses have been developed. These projects have ensured that the construction of any river barrier is accompanied by the construction of devices such as fish ladders, rocky chutes and shelters in order to preserve, as far as possible, the natural conditions required by the fish. Sanctions are applied to those who try to contravene the regulations of these projects.
- As far as possible incorporate the system of protection of endangered species of fish, protection of entire fish families and protection of fish-production capabilities of open water biotopes into the fishing industry. This is the only way to ensure that the protection system operates effectively. The protection of the ichthyofauna and fishing interests are identical, and therefore both professional fishermen and recreational anglers should be equally concerned with fish protection.
- The system of protection of ichthyofauna and especially the endangered species of fish must be founded on appropriate legislative regulations. These regulations should specify the terms of protection of fish fauna and the fish-

171

Artificial breeding has become the basis of preserving and maintaining the required numbers of economically important species of fish. The release of sexual secretions (spawn, milt) can be stimulated with the aid of hormones. This is carried out by injecting the hormones into the musculature of the female fishes.

Artificial spawning was originally only carried out in salmonids, for example in the female Rainbow Trout as illustrated in the picture. Nowadays most economically important species of fish are bred artificially.

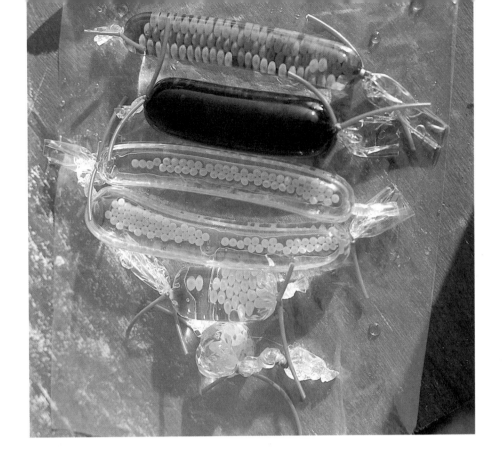

The transport of spawn and fish fry in plastic bags filled with an oxygen atmosphere.

ing allowances, and should include sanctions and fines if these measures are not fulfilled or are breached. The legislative regulations should also contain a list of the most endangered species of fish and their economic value, including a scale of fines if these fish are destroyed.

Proof that the problems of the ichthyofauna of European fresh-water systems are the object of interest, both of specialized and administrative bodies and institutions as well as of the public at large, are the legislative regulations issued and implemented for this area.

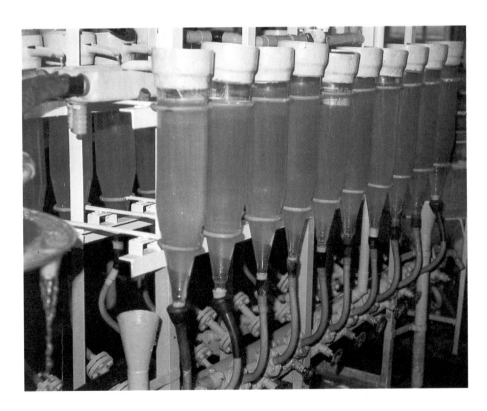

The hatching apparatus in bottle form, filled with the fertilized spawn of the Carp *(Cyprinus carpio)*.

Industrial fish hatcheries.

Various troughs, basins and tanks are used successfully to nurture hatched fry. With sufficient food, it is possible to feed and nurture a high density of fish fry. Here tanks are being used for feeding hatched Pike fry.

A fish-farm breeding Rainbow Trout and Brook Charr for human consumption.

Lists of the most endangered species have been issued in individual European countries. Although much has already been done, it is essential to maintain and increase our efforts in fish protection, in order to build a firm base for the future, both in ecological and economic terms.

As far as the outlook for the immediate future is concerned, it is generally assumed that, based on current knowledge, the species diversity of European ichthyofauna will not alter in any substantial way by the year 2000. The current efforts in the sphere of protection and breeding will, most likely, succeed in preserving even the most endangered species of fish. Apart from the already acclimatized species, it is unlikely that further species will be imported from different geographical regions. We must come to terms with the fact

175

Floating net cages anchored in large reservoirs and lakes are used for feeding Rainbow Trout.

that, particularly in the flowing waters, which are most polluted, the abundance and biomass of the economically important species of fish will decline. The numbers and biomass of those species which are ecologically and biologically flexible and resistant to unfavourable effects will most likely increase. Man's influence, and particularly that of the fishing industry, on the fish colonies of open water ecosystems will become increasingly important. As human society is the determining factor for the further development of the European ichthyofauna, man remains responsible for its fate. Future generations will judge how well our society has acquitted itself of this task.

The Fishing Industry

All of man's efforts concerning the capture of fish culminates in the fishing industry. Although on a worldwide scale, sea fishing is of the greatest importance in this sphere, the significance of fresh water fishing cannot be underestimated. The recent intensive exploitation of economically valuable species of fish in the world seas has substantially altered the original forecast about the inexhaustibility of sea fish supplies. Sea fishing has basically reached its peak. Now ever growing attention is being paid to the possibilities of increasing the stock and production of freshwater fish. At the present time the share of freshwater and draught species amounts to 16–19 % of worldwide catches, about 10 million tonnes of fish are taken from inland freshwaters. In future the share of freshwater fishing will increase. At pre-

The fish fry are the starting point for breeding young fish, or they are used directly for populating streams, lakes, rivers and reservoirs with fish.

sent freshwater fishing comprises several areas (based on the water systems used for fish production and breeding): fishing in open waters (lakes, water courses, valley reservoirs, pool, etc.) carried out by professional fishermen as well as so-called sporting anglers. The word 'aquaculture' refers to fish-farming (i.e. fish breeding in fishponds of various sizes and types – the Carp and Rainbow Trout form the main part of production) and then there are the industrial forms of fish breeding in modern aquacultural systems. This area of fishing is the youngest and its development started in contemporary times.

Conditions for the development of freshwater fishing vary greatly from one European country to another. In some countries fish-farming has its tradition and importance (e.g. the Czech Republic, Germany, Hungary, Poland), in others lake fishing is significant (e.g. Finland, Poland, Sweden), in countries where there are insufficient water areas for fish breeding, intensive industrial forms are being developed for the production of, for example, salmonids (e.g. Great Britain, Italy, France, Denmark). In all European countries angling is becoming an ever more popular sport.

Trout *(Salmo trutta)* fry for populating trout waters.

177

These small Carp have been marked with plastic tags before being introduced to a valley reservoir.

A-year-old Asps (*Aspius aspius*), nurtured in fishponds, will be used to populate rivers and valley reservoirs.

Angling

Some elements used in regulating water courses are of a natural character. This picture shows a so-called coarse slide, substituting the classic steps and weirs, and enabling fish to migrate against the water current thereby preserving the biological continuity of the water course.

Angling as a sport is gradually becoming one of the most important forms of fishing in the freshwater systems in Europe. The original purpose of fishing with a rod and line for economic purposes has taken on a further and equally important aspect, and that is fishing with a rod and line as a form of recreation. Nowadays angling is one of the most popular hobbies in most developed countries. Currently in Europe 20–22 million people, more than 4 % of the European population, are engaged in organized angling. The greatest number of anglers are found in Sweden (about 25 %), Finland (16 %) and France (10 %). The numbers are lower in other countries, 2 % in Bohemia, Moravia and Slovakia, and 1.1 % in Russia, for example. The number

179

All fishermen, whether professional or recreational, should be concerned with the conservation of clean rivers and healthy fish.

of potential anglers continues to increase, although in countries with a large population and sophisticated economy, the development of angling is being unfavourably affected by the increasing pollution of flowing waters (e.g. Belgium, Holland, Germany, France, Italy, the Czech Republic, Slovakia). Although its importance as a recreation is increasing considerably, angling has not lost its significance in economic terms. When the anglers put on enough pressure (1,000–2,000 hours of fishing per 1 hectare of water area annually) 100–250 kg of fish can be fished out of 1 hectare of open water with a rod and line. Fishing with a rod and line is a very effective method of extracting fish from water. For example, in France 30,000–70,000 tonnes of fish are extracted annually, in Poland about 15,000 tonnes, in Finland 10,000–12,000 tonnes, in former Czechoslovakia about 3,500 tonnes, etc.

In future it is likely that interest in angling will continue to grow in Europe especially in angling as a form of sport. Apart from the main motive – the acquisition of fish – other motives are gaining in importance – a relaxing sojourn in the open countryside and in a healthy environment, the sense of fulfilment and satisfaction gained with trophy catches, traditions, and so on. Most of these motives represent so-called recreational values and the importance of angling as a sport lies in the opportunity which it offers for relaxation in an otherwise stressful lifestyle.

The sport of angling also ensures the full utilization in economic terms of those open waters which cannot be put to use for intensive fish breeding. Although the system and organization of angling is different in individual countries, it has a number of common elements. Anglers represent an important pressure group, capable of stirring up society and campaigning for the improvement and protection of water purity. They are also an important part of the movement of nature conservationists. In a number of countries anglers are engaged in the rearing of fish fry which they release into safe waters and so significantly contribute to maintaining the optimum level of the fish populations.

Wonderful angling experiences should be the most effective stimulus in our efforts and struggle for preserving clean waters with a rich selection of fish, not only for ourselves, but for our children and descendants.

Fish Breeding

Fish breeding now forms the basis of freshwater fishing. The basic philosophy of fish breeding is aptly expressed by the Chinese proverb which says: 'Take fish and you will have a meal for the day, learn to breed fish and you will have enough food for the rest of your life.' Fish breeding has its longest tradition in the Far East. In China, India or Japan these traditions date back several thousands of years. As already stated, fish breeding in Europe is a much more recent tradition. The development of fish breeding has gradually led to the present situation, where this area, in many respects, has already acquired the status of industrial production, although its specific character is determined by the biological basis of this activity. This area of fishing has recently become known as aquaculture, which expresses very well the current state and level of the development of fish breeding. Man now manages and controls the production of fish, he intervenes in their environment, selects the level of intensity of fish breeding, refines and utilizes the most suitable biotechnical procedures, introduces and develops intensive and more sophisticated breeding methods for individual species of fish. Fish breeding in the current European freshwater fishing industry fulfils the following aims:

- it produces fish for consumption purposes (the most important aim)
- it undertakes the various development stages of fish (eggs, embryo, fry, maternal fishes) for the regeneration or improvement of fish populations in open waters
- it produces fish fry for the purpose of the fishing management of open waters
- it produces fish fry for angling – the 'give and take' system
- it produces new fish for the so-called unproductive fish populations where the fish fulfil a purpose other than a purely economic one – e.g. the elimination of aquatic plants by herbivorous fish, fish for maintaining good water quality in waterworks, reservoirs, etc.
- it fulfils fish production for fodder or technical purposes

Current fish breeding or aquaculture includes, above all, the classic form of fish production which is represented by fish-farming. Fish breeding in fishponds has preserved a certain typical character, although even here science, technology and modernization has also been implemented to intensify production. There has literally been an upheaval in fish breeding which has placed it on the level of domestic and farm animal breeding (cattle, pigs or poultry) and therefore has meant the incorporation of new biotechnological procedures into modern aquacultural systems. Fish breeding in cages, in metal or glass-laminated troughs, tanks and silos with regulated and controlled water quality, with a great number of fish and the relevant intensity of feed enables an annual production of 200–500 kg of fish per 1 m^3 of water. The operation of such large energy facilities (classic thermal and atomic plants, exchanger stations, etc.) generates a considerable amount of heated water to provide suitable conditions for the breeding and production of thermophilic species of fishes (e.g. the Eel, Carp – *Cyprinus carpio,* the Grass Carp – *Ctenopharyngodon idella*). It also contributes significantly towards fish reproduction, because it considerably shortens the time taken by the fish to reach sexual maturity.

One of the key areas in fish breeding is that of reproduction. It was not all that long ago that fish reproduction was a matter of natural spawning whereby fishermen only tried to create the most favourable conditions for fish to reproduce. Otherwise everything simply depended on nature, on the maternal fish, the weather, the conditions for spawning and the futher development of spawned eggs. So the effectiveness of reproduction formerly depended on these factors alone.

The first reports on artificial fish spawning were published in Germany in 1763 and 1765 by Jacobi who artificially spawned a Brown Trout *(Salmo trutta fario)*. Artificial spawning only began on a wider scale a hundred years later in the 19th century, when it became widespread throughout Europe and North America. Artificial reproduction was carried out, above all, on salmonids, as it was a fairly straightforward procedure to spawn the female Salmon – *Salmo salar,* the Brown Trout – *Salmo trutta fario,* Rainbow Trout – *Salmo gairdneri,* the Huchen – *Hucho hucho,* the Grayling – *Thymallus thymallus,* The Brook Trout – *Salvelinus fontinalis,* etc.). After the First World War artificial reproduction was practised on other fish – the Pike, the Carp and the Tench, resulting in a sudden expansion in artificial reproduction. In other species in the fishing industry it also meant the introduction of hormonal stimulation of ovulation in the female fish – the spawners, by injecting a suspension of fish hypophysis into the body – hypophysation. Hypophysation has enabled artificial spawning in virtually all species of fish. When the spawners are at their peak maturity, they are injected with the suspension of fish hypophysis (usually the hypophysis taken from the Carp is used), which contains the hormones necessary for the release of the eggs from the ovaries. At the right water temperature within 10–20 hours the eggs are released. The eggs can be pressed out by placing pressure on the abdominal cavity. These eggs are placed in bowls and spawned with the sperm (milt) of the male fishes. The eggs are fertilized after water is added and mixed. After removing any viscosity, the eggs are placed in special hatcheries.

Artificial fish reproduction has removed the fisherman's dependence on nature, it has achieved a substantial reduction in losses during egg incubation and regulated reproduction has led to the further intensification and development of fish breeding. For certain fish introduced to European waters, artificial reproduction is an essential precondition for their survival in European conditions – for example the Grass Carp *(Ctenopharyngodon idella),* the Silver Carp *(Hypophthalmichthys molitrix)* and Bighead Carp *(Aristichthys nobilis).* Further species – Whitefishes *(Coregonus lavaretus, Coregonus peled)* – can be utilized in fish-farming only thanks to artificial reproduction. Artificial reproduction is and will continue to be of key importance in the efforts to preserve and maintain endangered species in European waters. It is only thanks to artificial reproduction that we are beginning to breed and rear the fry of species which, until now, were not the object of fish production, but which form an important element in the fish colonies of open waters. So, for example, in the Czech Republic, artificial reproduction and rearing commenced of fry for populating rivers, lakes and reservoirs with such non-traditional species as the Barbel *(Barbus barbus),* the Nase *(Chondrostoma nasus),* the Chub *(Leuciscus cephalus),* the Orfe

(Leuciscus idus), the Asp *(Aspius aspius)* and the Burbot *(Lota lota)*.

Further processes follow the artificial reproduction in fish breeding, such as rearing fish fry to various ages, which are used either for the production of consumer fish or for populating open waters. A key role in fish breeding is played by maternal (generation) fish which lay the foundation for a new generation of fish. Hence fishermen focus their attention on these fish and complement their shoals with the best breeding fish. The complexities of modern fish breeding make great demands on the qualifications of fishermen and so the expertise of fishermen has developed to a correspondingly sophisticated level. Science and research, new technology and modernization have become characteristic elements of present-day fish breeding.

Currently fish breeding represents the foundation for freshwater fishing in Europe. Its further development will enable the establishment of many more sources of good quality animal proteins for human nutrition, the necessary fry for maintaining the optimum population level of open waters and will be of increasing importance for preserving the European ichthyofauna.

A Word in Conclusion

Man has always been the determining element or partner in his relationship with fish. Fish serve as his food, and they serve his hobbies. However, in his relationship with fish, man should always be aware that fish are living creatures whose survival depends on humanity. At the moment man is polluting their environment – the water, even though it is in his interest that the waters are kept clean and well populated with fish. It is said that a good fisherman is also a good person. So, in conclusion, let us be good fishermen.